A COUNTRY CHRISTMAS

Johnny Coppin is a singer/songwriter, formerly with the band Decameron, and appears regularly on television, radio and in concert. He has recorded many albums, and is best known for *Edge of Day* with Laurie Lee, *Forest and Vale and High Blue Hill*, and his most recent albums *Force of the River* and *A Country Christmas*. He is also the editor of two poetry anthologies *Forest and Vale and High Blue Hill* and *Between the Severn and the Wye*.

Anthologies by Johnny Coppin

Forest and Vale and High Blue Hill: Poems of Gloucestershire, the Cotswolds and Beyond

Between the Severn and the Wye: Poems of the Border Counties of England and Wales

A COUNTRY CHRISTMAS

An Anthology of Prose, Poetry, Carols, Songs and Folklore

SELECTED BY JOHNNY COPPIN

Line drawings by Jolyon Webb

THE WINDRUSH PRESS · GLOUCESTERSHIRE

For Gillian with all my love
and in memory of our dear friend Sue Herbert –
no one ever loved Christmas more

First published in Great Britain in 1996
by The Windrush Press
Little Window, High Street,
Moreton-in-Marsh
Gloucestershire GL56 0LL

Telephone: 01608 652012
Fax: 01608 652125

Introduction and Selection © Johnny Coppin 1996
The right of Johnny Coppin to be identified as editor of this work
has been asserted by him in accordance
with the Copyright, Designs and Patents Act 1988

Line drawings © Jolyon Webb 1996

British Library Cataloguing in Publication Data
A catalogue record for this book is available from
the British Library

ISBN 0 900075 77 5

Cover design by Chris Dawson
Typeset by Archetype, Stow-on-Wold, Gloucestershire
Printed and bound in Great Britain by The Lavenham Press Ltd., Suffolk

CONTENTS

INTRODUCTION

This anthology is very much a personal selection with the aim of capturing the spirit of a country Christmas. The mix of prose, poetry, folklore, traditional carols and original songs is based on my Christmas concert tours which began in 1990. Much of the material from the live shows has been included, with many of the songs and tunes from both my 'West Country Christmas' and 'Country Christmas' albums here in print for the very first time.

For as long as I can remember, I have always loved Christmas. In particular I love singing Christmas carols, and over the past few years I've enjoyed writing new carols and songs and arranging traditional material. Country traditions and folklore always fascinate me with their blend of both pagan and religious celebrations; from the beginning of Advent and Midwinter, through Christmas and New Year and on to Candlemas. Through my work with poets and writers such as Laurie Lee, Charles Causley, Thomas Hardy and Mary Webb, I have become increasingly appreciative of the great wealth of country writing. Their work captures the essence and character of country life, the good times and bad, with humour, with poignancy, and always with perception. It seemed only natural therefore to combine the carols and songs with prose, poetry and folklore as the basis of a Country Christmas collection.

I am indebted to many people for help with my research. A special thank you for prose, poetry and folklore to Paul Burgess and Lynn Holmes, along with Tony Kendall, Rex Hancy, John the Fish, the late Alan Hancox, Alan Rees, Betty Coy, Chris Smith and the staff of many libraries including: The Poetry Library in London, Cambridge, Leeds, Shrewsbury, Bristol, Bath, Gloucester, Dorchester, Keswick, Southampton, Leicester, Evesham, Lewes, and Exeter. For help with traditional carols and songs, a big thank you to Paul Burgess especially for scoring the music, and also to Simon Evans, Gloucester Local Studies Library, Sam Richards, Paul Wilson of the Wren Trust, Robert Patten, Vic Legg, Peter Kennedy, and Geoff Elwell. For their ideas and help with musical arrangements, a special thanks to Paul Burgess, John Broomhall, Phil Beer, Mick Dolan, Matt Clifford, Geoff March, Trevor Foster, and Gareth Sampson.

Thanks to Chris Dawson for cover design, and to Victoria Huxley and Geoffrey Smith of The Windrush Press for realising this anthology. Finally for continued support and encouragement, thanks to Gillian my guiding star, to all my family and friends, to members of my mailing list, concert promoters and followers everywhere.

I do hope you enjoy this anthology, and sharing the spirit of a country Christmas.

Keep the flame burning this Christmas,
Let the light shine out so clear,
Keep the flame burning this Christmastime,
Keep the flame burning all year . . .

JOHNNY COPPIN,
Gloucestershire, June 1996

ACKNOWLEDGEMENTS

The publishers would like to credit and thank the following for their kind permission in allowing the use of the poems and extracts in this anthology. While every effort has been made to contact the copyright holders the publishers would be happy to hear from anyone whom they have not been able to trace. The Literary Executor of Leonard Clark for 'Singing in the Streets' and 'Song for Loders' both by Leonard Clark (1972 Dobson Books); Winifred Foley for an extract from *Back to the Forest* (1981 Macdonald) and *A Child in the Forest* (BBC 1974); John Murray (Publishers) Ltd for an extract from *A Yeoman's Farmer's Son: A Leicestershire Childhood* by H. St G. Cramp; Sheil Land Associates for an extract from *A Magic Apple Tree* by Susan Hill, published by Hamish Hamilton © Copyright 1982 by Susan Hill; Laurence Pollinger Ltd for 'The Great Snow' by H.E. Bates; Duckworth Ltd for 'At Basingwerk Abbey' from *A Glass Island* (1992) by Gladys Mary Coles; Hodder & Stoughton Ltd for extracts from *The Secrets of Bredon Hill* by Fred Archer (1971 Hodder & Stoughton); Penguin Books for an extract from *Village Diary* Miss Read (Michael Joseph, 1957 © Miss Read 1957); The Windrush Press Ltd for an extract from *A Portrait of Elmbury* by John Moore; The Estate of Mollie Harris for an extract from *Another Kind of Magic* published by Oxford University Press; Roger Mason for an extract from *Granny's Village* published by Peter Davies Ltd 1977; Oxford University Press for an extract from *A Country Calendar* by Flora Thompson and to Random House (UK) Ltd for an extract from *Peverel Papers* by Flora Thompson; Peters, Fraser & Dunlop Group Ltd for an extract from *The Season of the Year* by John Moore published by Alan Sutton Ltd; Peters Fraser & Dunlop Group Ltd for an extract from *Cider with Rosie* by Laurie Lee published by Penguin; Margiad Evans for 'Over the Snows' from *A Candle Ahead* (Chatto & Windus) 1956; Random House (UK) Ltd for an extract from *Kilvert's Diary* ed. William Plomer (Jonathan Cape Ltd); The Dalesman for an extract from *Lakeland Ghosts* by Gerald Findler (1979); Alison Hodge for an extract from *When I set out for Lyonesse* by Judith Cook (1984); Victor Gollancz for an extract from *Country Matters* by Ian Niall (1984); David Higham Associates for poems by Charles Causley from *Collected Poems* published by Macmillan; David Higham Associates for an extract from *Let Sleeping Vets Lie* by James Herriot published by Michael Joseph; Coppersongs for an extract from *Early to Rise – A Sussex Boyhood* by Bob Copper (Heinemann 1976); Random House (UK) Ltd for 'Christmas' by W.H. Davies published by Jonathan Cape; David Higham Associates for an extract by Dylan Thomas from *Miscellany* published by J.M. Dent (1963); David Higham Associates for an extract from *A Solitary Landscape* by Edward Storey published by Victor Gollancz (1975); Sue Ryder Foundation for *A Cotswold Rag-Bag* by Bert Butler (1984); Brandon Book Publishers for an extract from *The Night Before Christmas* by Alice Taylor; Robert Hale Ltd for an extract from *Buckinghamshire Country Series* by Alison Uttley; HarperCollins *Publishers* Limited for 'Christmas Thank-Yous' from *Swings and Roundabouts* by Mick Gowar; Victor Gollancz for an extract from *Cumberland Heritage* by Molly Lefebure (1970); Hodder & Stoughton Ltd for an extract from *Wild Honey Time* by M. O'Donoghue (1972); Constable Publishers for an extract from *Hodingham Harvest* by Geoffrey Robinson (1977); Oxford University Press for 'Twelfth Night' by Peter Scupham from *Selected Poems* 1972–1990 (1990); Sybil Marshall and Cambridge University Press for an extract from *The Fenland Chronicle* by Sybil Marshall (1967); Mrs Dorothy Gibson for 'January' by Douglas Gibson from *Oxford Book of Christmas Poems*. The editor would also like to acknowledge his use of the following source material: *British Calendar Customs, England* by Wright and Lones (Folklore Society 1940); *British Calendar Customs, Scotland* by Mrs M. Macleod Banks (Folklore Society 1941); *The Book of Days* ed. R. Chambers. 1862; *Old English Customs* by P H Ditchfield (1901 Methuen); *A Celebration of Christmas* by Gillian Cooke (1980 Queen Anne Press/Macdonald Futura); *Saints in Folklore* by Christina Hole (G. Bell & Sons 1966); *Folklore and Customs of Rural England* by Margaret Baker (David & Charles 1974); *Folklore of East Anglia* by Enid Parker (Batsford 1974); *Cambridgeshire Customs and Folklore* by Enid Parker (1969 Routledge, Kegan and Paul); *The Folklore of Gloucestershire* by Roy Palmer (Westcountry Books 1994); *Customs and Folklore of Worcestershire* by Lavender M Jones (Estragon 1970); *Shropshire Folklore* by Charlotte Burne 1883; *Shropshire Folklore, Ghosts and Witchcraft* by Jean Hughes (Westmid Supplies 1977); *Somerset Folklore* by Ruth Tongue (Folklore Society 1965); *The Customs, Superstitions and Legends of Somerset* by C H Poole 1877; *Folklore of Herefordshire* by Ella Mary Leather (S. R. Publishers 1970); *Apple Games and Customs* by Common Ground 1994; *Ghosts & Legends of the Dorset Countryside* by Edward Waring (Compton Press 1977); *A West Country Christmas* by Chris Smith (Alan Sutton 1989); *Muker: The Story of a Yorkshire Parish* by Edmund Cooper (1948 Dalesman); *Some Christmas Customs and Carols* by Clarence Daniel (Derbyshire); *The Folklore of the Lake District* by Marjorie Rowling (1976 Batsford); *The Folklore of the Scottish Highlands* by Anne Ross (1976 Batsford); *Wiltshire Folklore* by Kathleen Wiltshire (1975 Compton Russell); *Lincolnshire Folklore* by Ethel H Rudkin (1973 EP Publishing Ltd); *Wit, Character Folklore and Customs of the N. Riding of Yorkshire* by Richard Blakeborough 1898; *Guising and Mumming in Derbyshire* by S O Addy (1907 Derbys. Arch Journal); *Mysterious Wales* by Chris Barber (1986 David & Charles).

SINGING IN THE STREETS

I had almost forgotten the singing in the streets,
Snow piled up by the houses, drifting
Underneath the door into the warm room,
Firelight, lamplight, the little lame cat
Dreaming in soft sleep on the hearth, mother dozing,
Waiting for Christmas to come, the boys and me
Trudging over blanket fields waving lanterns to the sky.
I had almost forgotten the smell, the feel of it all,
The coming back home, with girls laughing like stars,
Their cheeks, holly berries, me kissing one,
Silent-tongued, soberly, by the long church wall;
Then back to the kitchen table, supper on the white cloth,
Cheese, bread, the home made wine,
Symbols of the night's joy, a holy feast.
And I wonder now, years gone, mother gone,
The boys and girls scattered, drifted away with the snowflakes,
Lamplight done, firelight over,
If the sounds of our singing in the streets are still there,
Those old tunes, still praising;
And now, a lifetime of Decembers away from it all,
A branch of remembering holly stabs my cheeks,
And I think it may be so;
Yes, I believe it may be so.

LEONARD CLARK

STIR-UP SUNDAY
& EARLY DECEMBER

'Stir up, we beseech thee,
the pudding in the pot . . .'

'STIR UP SUNDAY'

The preparations for Christmas traditionally begin with the making of Christmas puddings in late November, in the week following 'Stir-up Sunday' – the last Sunday before Advent. The name comes from the Collect for the day 'Stir up, we beseech thee, the wills of thy faithful people . . . ', and many people remember the traditional rhyme:

'Stir up, we beseech thee, the pudding in the pot,
And when we all gets hungry, we'll eat the blummen lot.'

Everyone in the family should take turns to stir the pudding mixture, and woe betide anyone who spills any as this is a sign that they will be prevented in some way from eating any! The tradition is to stir 'three times three' with a wooden spoon in memory of the manger, and from east to west, like the sun and the three wise men. In Sussex and many other parts of the country, each member of the family could wish three times, but only one wish was ever granted.

A sixpence, a ring, and a thimble were stirred into the mixture to bring wealth, matrimony and 'single-blessedness' to whoever found them in their piece of pudding on Christmas Day. This idea of putting silver charms into the pudding may well relate to an earlier tradition of putting beans in the Twelfth Night cake. Christmas cake first appeared in the mid-nineteenth century, and is really only a more solid version of the pudding made suitable for a family tea.

Ah, wen I wur a girt hard bwoy,
We appetite nar mossel coy,
Tha baste thing out ta gie I joy
Wur a girt big figgety pooden . . .

EDWARD SLOW

Thirteen ingredients were used in puddings and mincemeat, in memory of Christ and his disciples. Sometimes thirteen puddings were made – 'one for every month and one for Judas' – with the Judas pudding left to go mouldy, or given to a passing tramp or gypsy. Among other superstitions, it was widely believed that if a Christmas pudding was cracked, the person who first eats of it would have a bad illness and die, and at Terrington St John, near King's Lynn in Norfolk, it was the custom for the coachman to give a piece of pudding to all the horses, cats and dogs to bring good luck the next year.

The country writer Winifred Foley has some vivid memories from her native Forest of Dean, and well remembers the great Christmas pudding theft:

THE GREAT CHRISTMAS PUDDING THEFT

Primitive tribes are often credited with better manners than their superiors. In our backwater little village we children were brought up strictly to be polite and to respect our elders.

All the same, I did not have to say 'hello' to Ferretty as he came into view with his lurcher dog and his pocket bulging with a ferret. He was not walking on the path. True to his character, he was taking a devious route between the tall thick ferns. If he got near enough I would practise my monkey-face on him, and serve him right! I took my attitude from the grown-ups. Ferretty was a thief; we all knew that.

Since his major crime, stealing Mrs. P.'s Christmas puddings, he had been mentally hung, drawn and quartered and sent to Coventry by his neighbours. Now he became the guilty peg on which to hang the blame for stolen cabbages, missing hens, and sometimes even their eggs. Had he not trained his lean lurcher dog to sneak into hen-runs and bring the eggs out unbroken in his mouth? He was as sly as mustard, and too fly to be caught in the act, but two and two could be put together. He would not work, but his wife and two children could eat meat most days, and it was not always rabbit that a curious nose might sniff roasting in their oven. He grew no onions himself, but plenty went into their stewpots. Suspicion became confirmation when from his own wife's mouth he was shown to be the pudding pincher.

Mrs. P. was perhaps the most respected woman in the village; a hard-working widow of impeccable character, who by her hard-earned shillings and frugal ways had brought up her family and never asked a crust from anyone. A few weeks before Christmas she made her puddings from ingredients scraped from savings throughout the year. Top-notch puddings they were; six of them, to last as special treats until the next Christmas. So rich were they in fruit and spices, they went almost black in the boiling. For their cooking she used the wash-copper in the back-kitchen built on the end of her cottage. She boiled them for eight or ten hours, gathering and chopping the fuel from the surrounding forest.

Late in the evening she flour-sprinkled six snow-fresh pudding cloths to re-cover the basins for their long storing. Then, lantern in hand, be-shawled against the cold, she went out to the copper to fish out her gourmet treasures. The long copper-stick poked nothing solider than the sides of the copper. Shocked, dismayed, and shaking with disappointment, she realised her puddings had been stolen. There was no policeman in our village; short of murder it would not have occurred to anyone to call on the services of one so high in rank. No-one had a touch of the Conan Doyle talents, either. The news brought suspicion, fury and disgust, and the vexed question of who could bring such disgrace to our village. Few other women made this festive luxury; now none would,

in case when put on the table it would arouse suspicion. Even the guiltless could not rest easy in their minds, for all knew the power of gossiping tongues.

Suddenly, months later, the mystery was solved. It came out during one of the heated rows that Ferretty and his wife indulged in. He must have driven her beyond the realms of caution, for she was heard to scream at him, 'I'll go an' tell Mrs. P. who stole 'er Christmas puddens!'

'An' doosn't thee ferget to tell 'er thous't 'elp to yut 'em.'

From now on the pair of them were ostracised, and the pity hitherto felt for the wife was dissipated. "Adn't thic good Mrs. P. brought up 'er own tin o' linseed meal an' clean rags to make poultices when Ferretty's little boy got the pneumonia? And 'adn't 'er sat up day an' night 'elpin' wi' the nursin' of 'im? Saved thic boy's life, that's what 'er done, an' that was the thanks 'er got for it!'

WINIFRED FOLEY

Late November was also the time for the country tradition of killing the pig in readiness for Christmas and the onset of winter. Here is a memory from Leicestershire:

When I was fifteen, I was five feet eleven inches tall, measured against the barn door, where notch after notch, each with a pencilled date, testified to my rapid growth. Like most growing boys, my thoughts dwelt often on food, and the abundance which Christmas provided was a warming prospect. The period of great plenty began with the late November pig killing. The exact time depended on the weather, the first killing coinciding with the first really cold snap. The second came in mid-December; and, when the family were all at home, there was a third in late January. So from November onwards, apart from renewing the larder with hams and bacon, we enjoyed all those delicacies which the pig so abundantly provides.

The November killing was really a sign to the whole village that Christmas was on the horizon. Forewarning of the event was spread abroad by our man who frequented The Crown Inn, and speculation began as to which villagers might participate in the spoils. Everybody knew there would be 'a little something' for the sick, the old or the very needy; also for anyone who had rendered us any special service during the year . . .

Service during the previous year was always rewarded even thought it might already have been paid for in cash or kind. Also, what Father considered 'decent conduct' was acknowledged. Who then was finally included? Jones for sweeping our chimneys; Larkin the roadman whose handiwork we witnessed daily at close quarters; Baker for returfing Grandfather's grave; Mrs Swingler for doing the Monday washing; Mrs Bagshaw for midwife services to Mother for several of us though the youngest of us was of school age now; the police sergeant for his zeal in keeping poachers off the farm . . . And so it went on.

The gifts varied subtly as to quality and quantity. The humblest gift was home-rendered lard or 'scratchings', those little nutty lumps left behind after the rendering of the lard. Ranking slightly higher were tripe, pig's chaps (cheeks) and 'trotters'. More rewarding cuts were a few chops, a pork pie, pig's liver and haslet. Each gift was wrapped in greaseproof paper and delivered on a white plate. Thus was the mutuality of village life recognised . . .

Father presided over the 'mystery' of pork pie making. Regularly each year we lost the recipe, handed down in the family for generations. Regularly Father discovered it deep in the bowels of his bureau, among land titles and tithe records. Annually, it became less decipherable, as the folded paper cracked along the seams. No one thought of making a copy. It was as if only the magic of the original recipe would produce the desired result. So annually we pored over the hidden secrets, divined the message and produced pork pies whose excellence I, and no doubt others, still remember.

The vital task of salting the bacon was also Father's job. It seemed to me to resemble embalming. Armed with salt and saltpetre, he would vanish into the pantry every evening for several weeks, like a high priest entering his holy of holies; there he performed his ritualistic rubbing. Only he, by some sixth sense, knew when the curing was just right and the hams and flitches ready to adorn the walls and beams of the kitchen, there to dry off completely, against the day of eating.

Daily we lived with the fruits of our labours. When we looked on the bacon in the kitchen, the hay in the rickstead, the milk in the churns, the apples in store, our morale was uplifted. Like the great Creator, we looked on our handiwork and it was good. The townsman might look down on us, his country cousins, but we pitied him. Tied too closely to a money economy, he lost half the joy of living, we thought. Paper money only, as a reward for labour, is truly but 'a promise to pay' – and one that is never fully redeemed.

from *A Yeoman Farmer's Son: A Leicestershire Childhood*
H. St. G. Cramp

Early December and the Beginning of Advent

Along with the preparations for the Christmas feasting, Advent is traditionally a time of joy and longing, a time for fasting, for Advent candles and calendars. It is also the time of some largely forgotten customs:

The Eve and Day of St Nicholas – 5–6 December

St Nicholas is the patron saint of children, the bringer of gifts, and the origin of Santa Claus and our own Father Christmas. In Holland and Belgium there is still a strong tradition of giving presents to children on the Eve of St Nicholas. In Britain and the rest of Europe, the 5 December also marked the start of the reign of the 'Boy-bishops'. In cathedrals, a boy was elected as 'Boy-bishop' to rule until the 28 December, and to undertake many priestly duties at services. His last day of office was celebrated by a procession through the town and blessing the assembled people. He then went on to a special dinner at which he had to preach a sermon. This old custom did not last beyond the reign of Mary in Britain, and the eighteenth century in Europe, although it was revived in some English parish churches with the 'Boy-bishops' only having minor duties, and certainly not preaching or taking services.

St Nicholas Fairs or Feasts are held at several villages in England. At Sydling St Nicholas in Dorset, a street fair was held until around 1700, with the tradition continuing to this day in the village hall. Susan Hill tells of one such feast held every year in her Oxfordshire village:

The Church, of course, doesn't mark Guy Fawkes night, but a few days before come those twin days of darkness and light, gloom and gladness, All Saints' and All Souls' Day, and early December brings Advent, and a special service in Barley Church on Advent Sunday, to mark the real beginning of Christmas, when the village children carry in candles, to provide the only light for the singing of the advent hymn.

December the sixth is the feast of St Nicholas and, as Barley Church is dedicated to him, there is a St Nicholas feast and in places of honour at the table that runs cross-wise to the other two are the choir, for St Nicholas is the patron saint of choirboys – though our church, like many another now, has as many girls as boys, as many ladies as men, in the parish choir. The feast takes place in the church itself. So does the Parish harvest supper. We set out trestle tables in an oblong shape, at the spacious back of the church, by the font and beneath the bell rope, which is tied up out of reach for the occasion. Choir parents, members of the Parochial Church Council and senior citizens of Barley are guests of honour, too, and everyone is served by the Women's Institute members and other parish ladies, who have prepared the food and drink in their own kitchens during the afternoon and brought it up in baskets. There are jugs of cider, and orange squash, there are cold meat pies and hot potatoes in their jackets, trifles and ginger cakes and bowls of nuts and sweets. The tables are laid with white cloths and decorated with holly from the churchyard and with wonderful chrysanthemums, great pom-poms of white and butter-yellow and rust red, grown by Mr Elder, who has won cups and trophies with them up and down the country for years. There is a grace, and a thanksgiving hymn sung by the choir, at their places, and a lot of laughter. It is an unusual occasion, personal to us, simple, joyful, traditional, the first of all the parties.

from *The Magic Apple Tree*
Susan Hill

Unusual Customs in Early December

On the 9 December, there used to be an old winter custom of celebrating robins. The robin and the wren were the symbolic birds of Beli and Bran, the sons of Gaia, the Earth Mother:

The Robin Redbreast and the Wren,
Are God's Almighty Cock and Hen

were quite overwhelmed, the lanes filled so as to be impassable, and the ground covered twelve or fifteen inches without any drifting . . .

A circumstance that I must not omit, because it was new to us, is, that on Friday, December the 10th, being bright sun-shine, the air was full of icy *spiculæ*, floating in all directions, like atoms in a sun-beam let into a dark room. We thought them at first particles of the rime falling from my tall hedges; but were soon convinced to the contrary, by making our observations in open places where no rime could reach us. Were they watery particles of the air frozen as they floated; or were they evaporations from the snow frozen as they mounted?

We were much obliged to the thermometers for the early information they gave us; and hurried our apples, pears, onions, potatoes &c. into the cellar, and warm closets; while those who had not, or neglected such warnings, lost all their stores of roots and fruits, and had their very bread and cheese frozen.

from *The Natural History of Selborne*
GILBERT WHITE

DECEMBER

While snows the window-panes bedim,
The fire curls up a sunny charm,
Where, creaming o'er the pitcher's rim,
The flowering ale is set to warm;
Mirth, full of joy as summer bees,
Sits there, its pleasures to impart,
And children, 'tween their parents' knees,
Sing scraps of carols o'er by heart.

And some, to view the winter weathers,
Climb up the window-seat with glee,
Likening the snow to falling feathers,
In fancy's infant ecstasy;
Laughing, with superstitious love,
O'er visions wild that youth supplies,
Of people pulling geese above,
And keeping Christmas in the skies.

On the Sunday after the 12 December, the 'Tin Can Band' at Broughton in Northants parades through the village at midnight making lots of noise with tin cans to frighten off the gypsies whose magic powers are feared. While at Ryhall in Rutland, the 16 December is St Tibba's Day. St Tibba was a local saint and patron of foulers and falconers, who celebrated her day at a shrine at St Tibba's Well.

The colder weather marks the beginning of winter and yet the change of season brings its own beauty to the country as Gilbert White describes:

As the frost in December 1784 was very extraordinary, you, I trust, will not be displeased to hear the particulars; . . . . The first week in December was very wet, with the barometer very low. On the 7th, with the barometer at 28 – five tenths, came on a vast snow, which continued all that day and the next, and most part of the following night; so that by the morning of the 9th the works of men

As tho' the homestead trees were drest,
In lieu of snow, with dancing leaves,
As tho' the sun-dried martin's nest,
Instead of ickles, hung the eaves,
The children hail the happy day –
As if the snow were April's grass,
And pleas'd, as 'neath the warmth of May,
Sport o'er the water froze to glass.

JOHN CLARE

H. E. Bates drew much inspiration for his work from the county of Kent, and here he poetica y describes the beauty of the country in the grip of a severe winter:

For the third year in succession winter fell on the same day. The long, wild, rainy autumn, the days of flying brown leaves herded by warm, wet sea-winds, broke at last on the Saturday before Christmas. The wind swung north: by afternoon it was very cold: by Sunday it was bitterly cold. By Monday the ponds were covered with ice that would bear, and by Tuesday there was snow. In 1939 it was snow such as no one had seen in England, so continuously at least and for so long, for fifty years and, in many places, for a hundred years.

That year there were many berries on the holly; in spring the trees everywhere had been covered by clusters of green – white, pink-touched blossom. There had been many berries, too, on the hawthorns, and there was a tree that stood claret-covered until the last week of December. The cold did not begin reluctantly, as it often does in England, but suddenly and bitterly and fiercely. It bit down on the earth like teeth. It bit with a black and scarring effect, so that the earth seemed skinned raw by wind and frost and the trees were bared down to the black bone of the branches. Then it began to snow with that mournful, silent beauty, steadily and relentlessly, that only a great storm of snow can give. There are sometimes wild and brief snows which merely pepper the ploughed land into bars of whiteness and shadow. But this snow covered everything. It came down without a break for a whole day, then for another day, and then for still another. For seventy-two hours, a day and night, it drove down on a bitter wind from a sky that seemed solid with dirty grey clouds as far as heaven itself. Almost always after great snow the sky clears. It becomes cloudless, more blue than summer, sun and snow dazzling as light from a flashed mirror. But now the sky showed no sign of clearing. The clouds remained thick and sombre, dirty as a vast sheepskin. For a day there was intense frost, then a thaw, then frost again, but the sky did not change. It remained always that sombre and dirty grey, as if it had in it a vast world of unfallen snow.

And everywhere the fallen snow was magnificent. Sometimes snow in England is a local story; this snow was a national epic. It piled deep in woods and lay like heavy froth on shrubs and trees. It filled to the brim the narrow roads that are carved in the steep sides of the downlands, so that they were still like rivers of snow running down the hill-sides long after the surrounding land was dark and unfrozen again and even touched with flowers. On the ridge below the Downs it drove through the hedgerows as if through gauze, and piled up on the western and southern sides of them in vast elongated drifts that blocked lanes and roads like miniature ranges of snow alps. The shapes carved by wind driving falling snow, and then by wind driving in bitter misty blizzards the light powder-snow refined by frost, were of fantastic splendour. They rolled away from the hedgerows like sea-waves of white marble. These waves were barbarously ridged, sharp-crusted, edged like knives. They were tipped with long and delicate curves which became overhanging eaves, making caves below. They were rippled like gigantic muscles of marble and into light branchings that were fringed like goose-feathers. They were as long and sharp as spears or as huge and deep and impassable as dunes of the purest snowsand. Wherever there were turns of road in high places, a bank, a hedge, a fence on the corner of unsheltered land, these drifts were shipped by ground blizzards into barriers of fantastic and lovely marble.

from *The Great Snow*
H. E. BATES

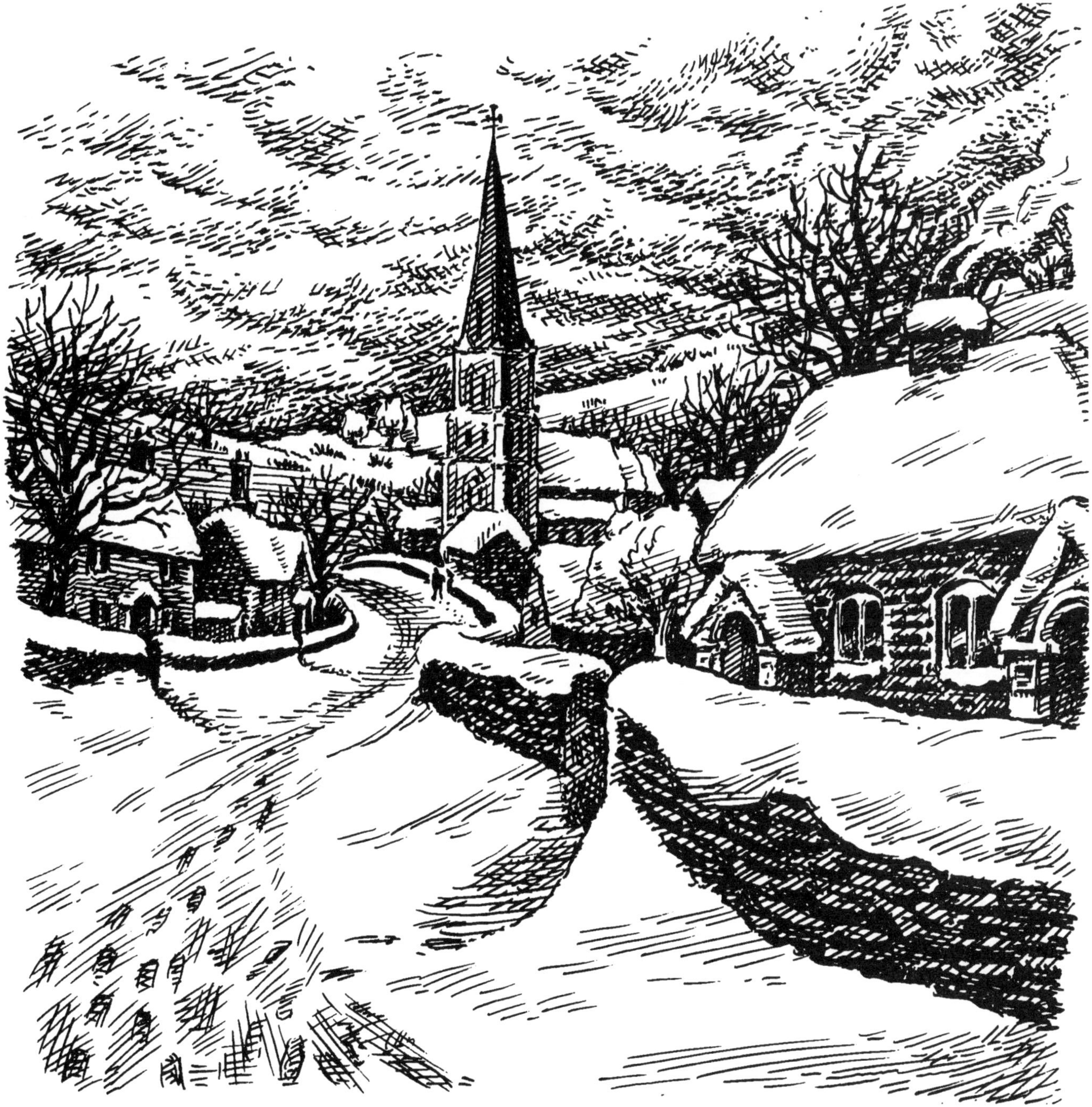

A SONG FOR LODERS

Words: Leonard Clark/Music: J. Coppin ©

2.   When mists fall low on Eggardon,
     And morning reddens sea and sky,
     From Vinney Cross to Powerstock
     The flocks of silent starlings fly,
     O, then, as evening breathes farewell,
     We take the rutted road to Bell.

CH. *So, up, my dear, and down, my dear,*
     The house is bringing Love tonight,
     And you, my dear, and you, my dear,
     Are trudging home in winter white.

3.   When stars shine clear on Eggardon,
     And field and fold are hushed with sleep,
     From Yondover to Askerswell
     The lanterns burn for wandering sheep,
     O, then, for us those lanterns burn,
     And, one by one, we shall return.

CH. *So, swing, my dear, and chime, my dear,*
     The tower is ringing Love tonight,
     And you, my dear, and you, my dear,
     Are trudging home in winter bright.

An evocative winter poem by Leonard Clark for the village of Loders near Bridport in Dorset. The names of the surrounding hills and villages are very English and full of images.

WINTER SOLSTICE

'St Thomas Gray, St Thomas Gray,
Longest night and shortest day'

WINTER SOLSTICE

The 21 and 22 December is the time of the Winter Solstice when the sun, the true country god of life, begins to climb the sky – to herald the return of longer days and the turning of the year towards Spring and Summer.

St Lucy (or Lucia) is one of the saints of the solstice. Before the reform of the calendar in 1752 (from Julian to Gregorian), St Lucy's Day, 13 December coincided with the winter solstice and this fact is still remembered in the old saying, 'Lucy-light, shortest day and longest night'. In northern Europe she is celebrated both as a martyr and a saint of the winter solstice in a feast of lights. In Sweden the day is sometimes called 'Little Yule' – when a young girl is crowned as the Lucia Queen and her procession visits all the houses and farms of the parish. Her presence drives out evil spirits and bad luck, and her candles symbolize the returning light of Spring. St Lucy's Eve was also a time for divining the future in Austria, Germany, and Denmark:

> *Sweet St Lucy, let me know*
> *Whose cloth I shall lay,*
> *Whose bed I shall make,*
> *Whose child I shall bear,*
> *Whose darling I shall be,*
> *Whose arms I shall lie in.*

This custom is very similar to one held on Guernsey, on St Thomas's Eve, 20 December.

20/21 DECEMBER
ST THOMAS'S EVE/ST THOMAS'S DAY

St Thomas, like St Lucy, is also a saint of light and darkness and his day marks the winter solstice. He is invoked for protection against witches and the forces of evil, and consulted on the future by divinations. On St Thomas's Eve one way was to throw a pair of shoes backwards over your shoulders, and leave them there without looking at them. If in the morning they were found pointing towards the door, it was a sign that their owner would leave home or marry during the coming year. If they pointed inwards there would be no change of dwelling that year.

Girls in England also used to induce dreams of future husbands by peeling an onion, and sticking it with nine ordinary pins - eight round a central 'true love' pin. Then it was wrapped in a handkerchief, and placed under the pillow, while the following rhyme was recited:

> *Good St Thomas,*
> *Do me right,*
> *Let my true love,*
> *Come tonight,*
> *That I may see him*
> *Face to face,*
> *And in my arms*
> *His form embrace.*

Apple divinations for telling the future were usually practised at Hallow'een, but in Guernsey and other parts of the Channel Isles, a girl could discover the identity of her future husband by passing two new pins crosswise through a Golden Pippin apple – or nine in the eye and nine in the tail of the apple. This then had to be wrapped in a stocking or garter taken from her left leg and placed under her pillow. She then got into bed backwards, whilst reciting a long incantation to St Thomas three times, and then did not speak another word. If the whole ceremony has been performed correctly she would then dream of her future husband!

In Yorkshire, St Thomas's Day was avoided for weddings as it was thought to be unlucky, the shortest day being an omen of a short married life. However in Lincolnshire it was sometimes deliberately chosen because the few hours of daylight left less time for a couple to repent their marriage!

St Thomas's night, the longest of the year, is the night when ghosts in a locality are said to gather to elect a new king for the coming year:

AT BASINGWERK ABBEY, IN WINTER

St Thomas' night. I tread the meadows – cold
white grass underfoot; sheep, ochre in the fold.
I walk alone among the abbey stones,
the broken cloisters, rosaries of bones.

Is that shadow or monk in the transept?
Does a hand move the worn, studded door?
Whispered vespers or night breeze?
Footsteps or mouse on the altar floor?

I hear madrigals in the rag-leaved trees,
wind wraps around the ruins –
through the bark-boned building, there
winding up the winding stair.

Where white-gowned monks no longer are
their orisons at break of star
rustle now among dry thistles.

GLADYS MARY COLES

THE TRADITION OF GOING 'A THOMASSING', 'GOODING', OR 'MUMPING'

Poorer children and villagers used to go from door to door begging for food or other gifts, and in return they would give sprigs of evergreen.

An old quête or collecting song sung by children ran:

Holly and ivy
Mistletoe bough,
Give me an apple,
And I'll go now.
Give me another
or my little brother
And I'll go home,
And tell father and mother.

In some areas such as East Anglia, older widows and widowers called at the more prosperous houses for donations. Even as late as 1942 one old lady at Haddenham, Cambs. went 'A-Thomassing' in the village, but more in affection for the old custom rather than being in need. In the village of Doddington the custom was known as 'Gathering Day' and each villager announced his presence by saying 'I've come gathering'.

Remnants of an earlier Mumming tradition occurred until 1914 at Barton, where boys called 'Mummers' blackened their faces and paraded the village saying 'Mum, mum, mum, dad, dad, dad, if you give me a ha'penny I'll be glad . . . ' and also at Grantchester, where black-faced boys known as 'Mumps' hit the ground outside houses with thick sticks crying 'Mump, mump, mump, if you don't give me a penny, I'll give you a thump!'

At Ellesmere in Shropshire the tradition was called 'clogging', and at Clun the 21 December was known as 'Clog-fair day'.

In Gloucestershire the custom was widespread. At Bitton near Bristol children chanted:

> Please, I've come a-gooding
> To buy m' mother a Christmas pudding

but in Willersey, Glos. by the early 1920s only children were involved and their rhyme was:

> Please to remember St Thomas's Day,
> St Thomas's Day is the shortest day.
> Up the stocking and down the shoe,
> If you an't got no apples money'll do.
> Up the ladder and down the wall,
> A peck o' apples'll serve us all.

At Arlesey in Bedfordshire, widows went round saying 'Please remember the Goodening'. In Cornwall, old women known as 'Christmas widows' used to collect money or ingredients for their 'bit of Christmas cake', and in Cheshire the custom of going from door to door was called 'curning' – with some villagers competing in 'yawning for a Cheshire cheese' – a version of 'gurning' or pulling faces.

In many parts of Britain this tradition involved collecting corn or flour. In Warwickshire, the custom was called 'going a-corning' because the villagers carried bags in which they received gifts of corn from the wheat growers, while at Duffield in Derbyshire, children used long bags or bolster slips to collect dry goods like oatmeal, sugar or rice; after each donation the bag was tied with string until eventually it resembled a string of sausages. In Herefordshire, farmers added a four pound measure of corn to the gleaners' pickings from the autumn fields and this was ground free by the miller for Christmas loaves. Shropshire farmers used to fill sacks with wheat for the poor and the flour was used for the Christmas bread. In Clun, cottagers were given wheat for themselves and barley for their pigs but from 1870 the charity corn was sent to the Town Hall for distribution and this continued until last century. At Aston Blank and St Briavels in Gloucestershire, corn was donated for frumenty or to be ground for flour.

In many parts of the country older people were given gifts of money collected and distributed by the local clergy. This was known as 'St Thomas's Dole'. At Eaton Bray in Bedfordshire, by the will of Hugh Cooke in 1634, an annual gift of thirty fourpences was established for widows in the parish – this was known as 'the Widows' Groats'. Other goods were also donated on St Thomas's Day. For example at Taunton, Somerset grocers gave complimentary goods and calendars to cheerful country shoppers in from the villages by gig or on horseback. At Kendal in Cumbria, old men were given blue cloth coats, trousers, calico and shirts, while the women received grey dresses, woollen shawls and black silk bonnets. At Holbeck in Yorkshire, churchwardens handed out calico, blankets, sheets and petticoats, while at Ambleside a lady once gave to the poor and widows of the town: 12 tons of coal, 4 fat rams, 30 stone of potatoes, and 46 loaves of bread! At Old Bolingbroke near Boston, Lincs, an unusual custom was a Candle Auction held to determine the next year's tenant of a piece of land, with the funds raised being distributed to the poor.

Here country writer Fred Archer shares with us some of his memories of Christmas preparations around St Thomas's Day in the villages under Bredon Hill in Worcestershire:

About a week before Christmas Day winter tightened its icy grip. 'Too hard to plough, Master Abel,' George said as he tried once more to move the rock-like ground with a new plough-share. His plough, frozen in the ground, he first thawed out by lighting a bolting of straw under the shield board. Joe Bradfield found it hard to move his sheep hurdles.

Arthur Jones, in his first winter on the land, cried with chilblained feet and hands as he carted more fodder, more litter, in the muck cart over frozen ruts.

The schoolboys and girls slid on the moat pond. They slid in the moonlight and lantern light after tea.

On the day the school broke up for the holiday the Governess, helped by the farmers' wives, gave tea and entertainment for the pupils. 'A bun struggle,' Bill Bowman called it, when his grandchildren came back with their oranges and cakes.

The berried holly was tempting food for the birds. George Bowman cut some off the hill for Abel's dining room. Boys climbed the gnarled cider apple trees at Bumbo for mistletoe and sold it to the Evesham shops.

Emma Bowman plucked Christmas geese until the late hours.

Jim Bowman bought a cockerel for Catherine's family in Evesham.

The Ashton farmers bought a side of beef from Collins at Evesham. This was jointed for all the families on the land.

David Ricketts from Fred Burford's was put off work temporarily because of the weather. His brother looked after the stock. David followed the threshing machine for ten days, from farm to farm carrying his shuppick,

pitching boltings at half a crown a day. Then just a few days before Christmas he joined one of the Baker's with a melodeon and they sang carols all round Bredon Hill.

The Russians came with their dancing bear to the White Hart. One Russian kept his bear in Syd Jackson's pigsty. Two men from the village near by went up at night to steal a sucking pig. Confronted with the bear they ran hell for leather down from the wood.

German bands played outside the pubs. The uniformed bandsmen slept in stables and tallets; Tewkesbury drum and fife band played on wintry nights at the bigger houses.

'Oh come all ye faithful . . . ' The Christmas spirit was spreading over a poor village, where the children who were lucky got a penny, an orange and a sugar mouse in their stocking.

The servant girls in the farmhouses stoked the furnace while basins of Christmas puddings boiled in the copper . . .

The women took the youngsters to Beckford on St Thomas Day to chant their little piece around the big houses. They were asked in as usual as they sang, 'Bud well, bear well, God send fare well a basket of apples to give on St Thomas morning.' Then out came the cakes and sweetmeats for the youngsters and the mumping money for their mothers.

Then they went to the school where Mr Smith the stores had all the material on purpose for winter use laid out: red flannel and shirts and socks for the men. Here they spent their mumping money, also charity money the parson doled out to such as deserved it.

Then there was a bread fresh baked.

'All they do at Ayshon,' George said, 'is the ringers ring the bells about six o'clock in the morning on December 21st, St Thomas Day, then the youngsters come round singing, "Here we come a Thomasin', a Thomasin', a Thomasin,' Here we come a Thomasin' so early in the morning." The people as can afford it give them pennies.'

from *The Secrets of Bredon Hill*
FRED ARCHER

TRADITIONAL YORKSHIRE CAROL

We've been awhile a-wandering
Amongst the leaves so green,
But now we come a-wassailing,
So plainly to be seen . . .

For it's Christmas time,
When we travel far and near;
May God bless you and send you
A happy New Year.

We are not daily beggars
That beg from door to door;
We are your neighbours' children
For we've been here before . . .

We've got a little purse,
Made of leathern ratchin skin;
We want a little of your money
To line it well within . . .

Talking of children, we must not forget that schools start their Christmas holiday usually just before the Winter Solstice. All the excitement of the end-of-term party is evoked in this extract from the *Village Diary* of Miss Read from Berkshire:

By right and ancient custom at Fairacre School the last afternoon of the Christmas term is given up to a tea-party.

The partition had been pushed back, so that the two classrooms had been thrown into one, but even so, the school was crowded, with children, parents and friends . . .

It was a cheerful scene. The paper-chains and lanterns swung from the rafters, the tortoise stoves, especially brilliant today from Mrs Pringle's ministrations, roared merrily, and the glittering tree dominated the room.

The children, flushed with food, heat and excitement, chattered like starlings, and around them the warm, country voices of their elders exchanged news and gossip.

After tea, the old well-loved games were played, 'Oranges and Lemons' with Miss Clare at the piano, and Mr and Mrs Partridge making the arch, 'Poor Jenny sits a-weeping', 'The Farmer's in his Den', 'Nuts and May' and 'Hunt the Thimble'. We always have this one last of all, so that we can regain our breath. The children nearly burst with suppressed excitement, as the seeker wanders bewildered about the room, and on this occasion the roars of 'Cold, cold!' or 'Warmer, warmer!' and the wild yelling of 'Hot, hot! You're REAL hot!' nearly raised the pitch-pine roof.

The presents were cut from the tree, and the afternoon finished with carols; old and young singing together lustily and with sincerity. Within those familiar walls, feuds and old hurts forgotten, for an hour or two at least, Fairacre had been united in joy and true goodwill.

It was dark when the party ended. Farewells and Christmas greetings had been exchanged under the night sky, and the schoolroom was quiet and dishevelled. The Christmas tree, denuded of its parcels, and awaiting the removal of its bright baubles on the morrow, still had place of honour in the centre of the floor.

Joseph Coggs' dark eyes had been fixed so longingly on the star at its summit, that Miss Clare had unfastened it and given it into his keeping, when the rest of the children had been safely out of the way.

The voices and footsteps had died away long ago by the time I was ready to lock up and go across to my peaceful house. Some of the bigger children were coming in the morning to help me clear up the aftermath of our Christmas revels, before Mrs Pringle started her holiday scrubbing.

The great Gothic door swung to with a clang, and I turned the key. The night was still frosty. From the distant downs came the faint bleating of Mr Roberts' sheep, and the lowing of Samson in a nearby field. Suddenly a cascade of sound showered from St Patrick's spire. The bellringers were practising their Christmas peal. After that first mad jangle the bells fell sweetly into place, steadily, rhythmically, joyfully calling their message across the clustered roofs and the plumes of smoke from Fairacre's hearths, to the grey, bare glory of the downs that shelter us.

I turned to go home, and to my amazement, noticed a child standing by the school gate.

It was Joseph Coggs. High above his head he held his tinsel star, squinting at it lovingly as he compared it with those which winked in their thousands from above St Patrick's spire.

We stood looking at it together, and it was some time before he spoke, raising his voice against the clamour of the bells.

'Good, ain't it?' he said, with the utmost satisfaction.

'Very good!' I agreed.

from *Village Diary*
MISS READ

St Thomas's Day was also one of the days of the year for the custom of 'barring out the schoolmaster', although this was perhaps more to do with the end of school term than with St Thomas. Children rushed to school ahead of their teacher, and locked and barricaded the door until he or she had promised them an immediate holiday. The children defended the barricade with shouts or songs of defiance. A Scottish example ran:

This is the shortest day,
An' we maun hae the play;
An' if ye wunna gies the play,
We'll steek ye oot a' the day.

PLANT AND WEATHER LORE

At Harvington in Worcs. they wassailed the apple trees on St Thomas's Day rather than at New Year with this song:

Wassail, wassail, about the town,
Got any apples throw them down,
Jugs white, ales brown,
This is the best house in our town.
Holly and ivy and mistletoe bough,
Give me an apple and let me go.
Up the ladder and down the wall,
Up the stocking and down the shoe,
Got no apples, money'll do,
Got no money God bless You!

In the south of England broad beans should be planted on this day, and wise gardeners should check the skin of their onions to determine the winter weather as in an old Cotswold saying:

Onion skins very thin
Mild winter coming in.
Onions skins thick and tough
Coming winter very rough

FINAL PREPARATIONS AND CHRISTMAS MARKETS

The 22 and 23 December is the time for the final preparations for Christmas – a time for the killing of beasts and poultry, the Christmas markets, and the making of mincemeat and pies. In Ireland on the Saturday before Christmas, Irish families 'bring home the Christmas' – with geese, turkeys, fresh produce, bread, sweets, biscuits, whisky, wine and beer. Here John Moore gives us a wonderful description of a typical English country Christmas market:

CHRISTMAS FAIR

There was one day that fell in early December, more exciting than Christmas itself; the day of Christmas market. Always on this occasion my father's firm provided sandwiches and drinks for all comers: dealers, smallholders, cowmen, shepherds, drovers. (The more substantial farmers were entertained to luncheon at the Swan.) Great were the preparations on the day before the market. Enormous joints sizzled in Old Cookie's oven; baskets of loaves lay everywhere about the kitchen, huge pats of yellow butter, tongues, sausages, pasties. Maids were busy all day cutting sandwiches, which were piled on dishes and covered with napkins. There was an air of bustle and festivity all over the house; but, alas, the festive spirit coupled with the near approach of Christmas was too much for Old Cookie; when the last joint was roasted, she got drunk. Lachrymose, incoherent, completely plastered, she confronted my mother and was given the sack. Next morning, sick and repentant, she was re-engaged.

Although the sale did not begin till half-past eleven, the first beasts began to pass our window as early as half-past nine. Thenceforward for two hours there passed down Elmbury High Street a procession such as might serve as a country counterpart of a Lord Mayor's Show. But here were no city financiers whose riches were scraps of paper locked in safes – riches which might disappear to-morrow if somebody else juggled with his shares more cunningly. Here was solid wealth, the real wealth of England, a sight that would have warmed old Cobbett's heart to see: fat oxen, sleek and ponderous, white-faced Herefords curly haired between their straight horns, Shorthorns as rich-red as the fresh-turned loam, dark as the winter ploughland where the sweat stained their sides; flocks of sheep, broad and flat-backed so that the collies could run about on top of them, thick-woolled, black-faced Oxfords, whose multitudinous breaths in the frosty air made a mist which moved as their great flocks moved like rivers down the street; and huge fat waddling pigs, sows whose bellies had brought forth great litters and which now brushed the earth between their short legs, bacons, porkers, Large Whites, Large Blacks, Middle Whites, blue-mottled cross-breds, sandy Tamworths, and the ancient dappled breed of Gloster Spots.

Here was the annual harvest of the great stock-fattening farms which lay in the rich valleys of the two rivers; here was a season's consummation, the happy outcome of the marriage between English weather and English soil, delivered by the skill and patience of men whose grandfathers had owned their farms before them. To this end the turgid waters of last winter's floods had left their rich alluvial deposit in the meadows, so that the spring grass sprang more greenly; to this end in Elmbury Ham in June, and in a thousand such great hayfields, sweaty men with pitchforks had built a village of sweet-smelling ricks; to this end swedes and turnips and mangel-wurzels, plump roots nearly as big as a football, had alternated in their proper rotations with golden corn and brown fallow on the slopes of the gentle hills which rose from the valleys. And now the purpose of all these labours was manifest. Down the street towards the market on slow hoofs waddled the Champion Beast, great-shouldered, broad-sided, deep-flanked; and a hundred more that were nearly his match. No man so poor that he would not taste a steak on Sunday; no family in such straits that they would not see a joint on their table on Christmas Day.

Just as the Lord Mayor's Show provides its moments of comic relief, so did this splendid progress towards the Christmas market. The calf that planted its legs foursquare and flatly refused to budge, though one man heaved at its halter and another pulled its tail; the fat goodwife with a couple of cackling geese under her arms; the bull which entered Double Alley and rampaged about there, so that even the Hooks made common cause against it: all these events were matters for mirth and jesting. And later in the day, when the market was over and the farmers with bulging pockets rollicked home – when the drovers rich with Christmas tips began their Christmas pub crawl – when the butcher who had bought the Champion Beast paraded him through the town with rosettes upon his horns, a mighty fat butcher with a mighty fat beast – what merry greetings passed, what practical joking went on! I shall never forget the butcher's face wreathed in smiles as he met Mr. Jeffs who had bred and fattened the champion; beaming at each other, they shook hands, and the crowd in the street cheered and shouted. I shall never forget the butcher's obvious pride that he had paid the highest price for the best animal. Nowadays, it seems to me, too many people take pride in having bought something cheap; but the butcher was proud because he had bought something good, and had paid well for it.

And so dusk fell, and the lamplighter went round with his long pole, the gas lamps glowed yellow, even that wan, cloudy nebulus that burned at the entrance to Double Alley, and the last of the country people went home. Only a few belated drovers still hung about the pubs; and the first carol-singers gathered round our front door to tell their old tale of peace on earth and goodwill among men.

from *Portrait of Elmbury*
JOHN MOORE

The tradition of killing a goose for Christmas was probably first introduced to Britain and Ireland at the time of Queen Elizabeth I, and very soon after turkeys were possibly first brought back to England from Mexico by William Strickland while on one of Cabot's explorations. He successfully farmed turkeys near Bridlington and presented one to Queen Elizabeth who enjoyed this novel food. Then when James I came to England he took a dislike to the traditional boar's head, and substituted it with turkey. It has remained popular ever since.

But we're running ahead of ourselves rather, and must wait till Christmas Day itself before enjoying Christmas fare. In the meantime, Mollie Harris shares with us a memory of 'turkey-rustling' somewhere deep in the Cotswolds:

'I didn't tell you about the bad luck our gaffer had just affor Christmas did I? Well, you know 'e breeds a lot of turkeys – dang me if 'e didn't have about sixty of 'is stock birds pinched. Ah'h, three nights running somebody broke in. So old Fred Bailey, the farm foreman, suggested that two fellows ought to be on guard every night, well until after Christmas anyroad.

'And 'e said that 'e and 'is son would take the fust night's watch. And according to them this is what 'appened.

''Twas cold and frosty as Fred and his son Dick donned thur old army great-coats and Wellingtons; they pulled thur caps well down over thur ears, laced thurselves with half-a-pint of ten-year-old dandelion wine and set off for the field, guns under thur arms.

'As they walked through the village they 'eard singing, coming from the pub it was too.

'"I'll bet tha's old Walt Tovey, I can recognise his melodious voice a mile off," Dick said. You see 'e was givin' 'um his special "Lille Marlene", and that being a clear frosty night made it sound louder. "We'd best get inside and 'ave half a pint 'er two affor we settles down hadn't us bwoy?" old Fred said, and thur was a roar of welcome as they went in; I knows cos I was set in thur with old Ned.

'"Come on and have half a gaiger with I," he called to

'um, "theet want summut in yer insides to keep you warm if you be going to spend the night out in that field."

'Arter they'd had three or four pints, all the foreman and his son did was brag about 'ow they was goin' to ketch the thieves red-handed. "We shall cop 'um tonight, you see if we don't, thur'll be no need for any of you others to keep watch, it'll all be over be mornin'," they said. "All we shall do is fire a few shots a bit low and scare the backside of 'um."

'They stuck in the pub till closing time, then made thur way off up to the field where the turkey arks was. It 'ad begun to snow – that nasty swirling blinding snow, the sort that gets you wet through in no time.

'"The best thing we can do" Fred said, "is to park ourselves somewur so as we can see 'um come in the gyet (gate) – they got to come that way, thur yent no other way to get in the field. We cyant stop out in this weather bwoy", Fred went on, "we shall get buried in the snow at this rate, let's see if we can fix up some shelter of some sort." Then Dick had a brainwave.

'"If we was tu get in this yer ark, we should 'ave a clear view if anybody come in the field and we should be in the warm too."

'So they snuggled down along with 'alf-a-dozen fat cock birds; 'twas warm and close in thur and they was soon fast asleep.

'Suddenly Fred woke up – for a few moments he couldn't make out where he was – then 'e nudged his son – "Hey wake up bwoy," he said, "we be on the move."

'They, turkey arks and all, had been pinched and was halfway to London on the back of a lorry.

'It was a few minutes before they realised what was going on. Then Fred said, "What be us tu do now then bwoy? Shall us lay yer quiet till they stops somewur, then we can hold 'um at gunpoint, we still got the guns."

'"I got a better idea," Dick said, "If they two in the front was tu stop and go into a café, I could slip out and fetch a policeman smartish quick an' bring 'im back yer affor they makes awf agin."

'After a while the lorry drew up in a grimy back-street, in a big town by the look of the buildings they thought.

Both of the men in the front jumped down and went into a house.

'"Go on bwoy, make a run for it", Fred whispered, "And dun't ferget tu find out the name of the strit we be in, else you wunt know were tu come back tu."

'Dick crept out of the ark and up the dimly lit strit. Twas about three o'clock in the mornin' and not many folk about. After walking up a couple of strits he saw a phone box, dialled 999 and asked for the police. The night duty copper listened at the wild tale that the fellow on the phone was telling him. Course he thought twas somebody having a joke.

'Then Dick said a bit urgent like, "If you dunt send somebody quick tu Fernstack Road thur'll be murder dun when they turkey thieves come up 'gainst my old man, I tell 'e you'll 'ave tu 'urry up else somebody's going' tu get hurt."

'"You stay where you are young man," the policeman said, "and I'll send a patrol car round to pick you up and take you back to Fernstack Road, and don't do anything silly like shooting anybody."

'By the time the police got thur old Fred had got the thieves up agen the wall. He'd got 'is 12-bore gun held a bit close to 'um and was swearing summut terrible at the lorry driver and 'is mate.

'The police took charge of the thieves and asked Fred and Dick to go to the station too, and they'd see as they go back home all right.

'Then one of the turkey thieves turned to Fred and Dick and said, "how the devil you come to be so 'andy, to be here at the same time as we, did you follow us all the way up here?"

'"We followed you all right, only you brought us, we was in one a they turkey arks."

'"Well, I'm b— " the other fellow said, "who'd a thought it, but now you comes to mention it, I thought that last b— ark we put on the lorry was damned heavy."

'Ah, we've had many a laugh over that,' Mark said, shaking his head and chuckling.

from *Another Kind of Magic*
MOLLIE HARRIS

In Yorkshire, Roger Mason remembers when a very welcome raffle prize was won at the village pub:

'Nay, Will,' said Mam, 'tha's not going out tonight.' 'Aye, lass,' said Bushman, it wasn't often he called Mam 'lass'. 'It's the grand raffle at t'Pickhill. Tha's not afraid to be left at home?' 'Don't be daft,' said Mam sharply and disapprovingly. 'You'd best be off.' Dad said 'Good night' and opened the door, letting in a howl of wind. After two steps the sound of his boots disappeared. The village pub had been closed when he was a boy and now he faced a two-mile walk in either direction simply to get a drink. Nelly and Annie, little girls still at eleven and nine, shuddered and looked at each other. How could Dad set off down the dark road to Elslack under the swaying black trees on such a night and after such a tale? They crept upstairs, whispering comfortingly, and got into bed. Next door the boys were wrapping their shirt-tails about their legs and being howling ghosts all over the room. Nelly shivered deliciously, thankful for having a warm house, a sister beside her, and neighbours in the village close by.

She heard Mam come upstairs, saw a flicker of candle-light from under the door, and heard the big bed creak as she got in and turned over. The house was quiet. She must have fallen asleep. Suddenly, there was a bang at the front door and footsteps below. Nelly and Annie shot up in bed and grabbed each other's hands. They sat still in the darkness, their hearts beating. Then they recognized the heavy tread on the stairs. It was only Dad, back from the Pickhill. He climbed slowly up in the dark and they heard him strike a match to light the candle next door.

Everything was all right and the girls began to settle down to sleep again. But then they heard a shriek from Mam, a smothered laugh from Dad, a sharp 'Now Will' and a little chuckle from Mam herself. The girls sat up, saw candlelight shining under the door, jumped out of bed and peeped into the front bedroom. Dad stood in the flickering candlelight still wearing his boots and coat. Over by the window they could see the boys' faces through the painted bars of their bed. They had turned over, rolled up to their ears in the crumpled bedclothes and were peering out above the striped bolster. Dad chuckled again and moved to the foot of the bed. The girls looked in amazement. What was that lying beside Mam on the bed? An enormous feathered thing. Why it was a goose, a great big goose with its neck hanging over the side of the bed and its bill almost touching the floor. 'Now, Will, the lasses are awake as well,' said Mam from under the bedclothes. Somehow Dad was not properly ashamed of himself. He turned and held out his hands to his girls. They stood together and admired the goose. 'It were t'first prize,' he explained, then, with proper pride and ceremony, Dad raised its fat body from the bed and walked downstairs to pluck the monster. The girls looked at their mother and she shook her head.

The giant goose in all its glory re-appeared for Christmas dinner, after a week spent hanging naked on the workshop wall. There it sat, golden and glowing, on a huge blue and white dish borrowed expressly from the Post Office, surrounded by a steaming pile of brussels sprouts. Dad took up the carving knife, Grandad stroked his beard in anticipation, Mam and Grandma smoothed their skirts and took a sip of rhubarb wine and the girls passed their plates across the crocheted table-cloth. They ate until only a skeleton remained on the dish and their chins were greasy with the good meat. Dad retold the tale of his triumphant entry with due exaggeration. Then Mam capped it by swearing that when first she opened her eyes she thought Will had grown a long white beard overnight. 'Oh, Mam, you didn't,' all the children groaned.

The plum-pudding came on in flames and was followed by tea and mince pies. Even little Alan could hardly move after his dinner and had to sit still for at least five minutes. It was already dark outside. Firelight shone on the whole family crowded into the front room. It caught the white cloth on the table and reflected them all in facets and angles of the cut-glass knobs on the dresser against the wall. Only the piano remained black and silent, waiting until they had wind enough to unlock its keyboard and fill the room with carols.

from *Granny's Village*
ROGER MASON

SNOW

In the gloom of whiteness,
In the great silence of snow,
A child was sighing
And bitterly saying: 'Oh,
They have killed a white bird up there on her nest,
The down is fluttering from her breast!'
And still it fell through that dusky brightness
On the child crying for the bird of the snow.

EDWARD THOMAS

MINCE PIES

Mincemeat had to be tasted by all – and, for every house in which a person eats a mince pie during the Twelve Days, he or she will enjoy a happy month in the coming year. Mince pies were made in twelves, and should be offered by a friend. Hence the old custom of offering a mince pie and a glass of wine to all visitors during Christmas, no matter what time of day. As in the making of Christmas puddings, thirteen ingredients were used in mincemeat. Mince pies were once known as 'shredded mutton pies' as they included meat of all kinds as well as raisins, sugar and spices. Originally they were oval-shaped to represent the cradle of the Holy Child and there were many regional variations – in Nottinghamshire farmhouses in 1850, families were given 'mince-pigs' with long snouts, curly tails and currants for eyes.

At one time there was an unusual custom at North Curry in Somerset. A feast was held in memory of King John, the chief dish among the pastry being a huge mince pie, decorated with an effigy of the King. Two candles weighing a pound each were lit, and for as long as they were burned, the visitors had the right to 'regale themselves with jolly good ale and old'.

HOUSE-CLEANING

Nothing was supposed to be dirty at Christmas time. Farmworker's wives were called in to help with cleaning the farmhouse and everything was scrubbed clean, before decorating with holly and ivy on Christmas Eve. Pewter and other vessels had to be so bright that maids could see to put their caps on in them, and they were often rewarded with a coin placed in a shoe! All soap-suds had to be out of the house by the end of Christmas Eve, as it was considered very unlucky to do any cleaning during the 12 days of Christmas. In the rural areas of many countries the days before Christmas were spent sweeping, and whitewashing farms and yards. In Norway the last Sunday before Christmas is still called 'Dirty Sunday'.

An idea of how important all this activity was comes from Charlotte Brontë's *Jane Eyre*:

'What aim, what purpose, what ambition in life have you now?'

'My first aim will be to *clean down* (do you comprehend the full force of the expression?) – to *clean down* Moor House from chamber to cellar; my next to rub it with bees-wax, oil, and an indefinite number of cloths, till it glitters again; my third, to arrange every chair, table, bed, carpet, with mathematical precision; afterwards I shall go near to ruin you in coals and peat to keep up good fires in every room; and lastly, the two days preceding that on which your sisters are expected will be devoted by Hannah and me to such a beating of eggs, sorting of currants, grating of spices, compounding of Christmas cakes, chopping up of materials for mince-pies, and solemnising of other culinary rites, as words can convey but an inadequate notion of to the uninitiated like you. My purpose, in short, is to have all things in an absolutely perfect state of readiness for Diana and Mary before next Thursday; and my ambition is to give them a beau-ideal of a welcome when they come.'

In Aberdeenshire all dishes were kept clean and empty on Christmas Eve. All scraps of food were given to pigs or poultry, and no bread was baked or clothes washed between Christmas Eve and Hogmanay.

It was also considered very unlucky to do any spinning during the 12 days holiday so the distaff or spinning wheel was put aside and decorated with flowers until St Distaff's Day. In west Shropshire, maids used to see how many 'slippings of yarn' they could complete before Christmas.

23 December – Tom Bawcock's Eve

Many Christmas customs are based around food and feasting, and at Mousehole in Cornwall, there's a particular dish they make to celebrate Tom Bawcock's Eve, 23 December.

The legend goes that, many years ago, as December had been an unusually stormy month, the fishermen had not been able to put to sea and, as a result, the people of Mousehole were starving. However, two days before Christmas, there was a slight lull in the storm, and one of the fishermen, Tom Bawcock, decided to risk everything and take his boat out to sea. Everyone in the village was sure that he would drown, but that same evening, his boat somehow struggled back into the harbour. On board he had a huge catch consisting of seven different types of fish, and more than enough to save the people of Mousehole from starving.

So, to commemorate this occasion, each year on the 23 December, a special pie is baked called 'Star-Gazey Pie'. The ingredients include potatoes, eggs, and seven different types of fish, and poking out of the pie-crust, are the fish heads, with their eyes gazing up to heaven.

CHRISTMAS EVE

'Make we merry, both more or less,
For now is the time of Christmas!'

LORD OF ALL THIS REVELLING

Words: Robert Herrick/Music: J. Coppin ©

1. What sweet- er mus-ic can we bring- Than a car-ol for to sing The birth of this our heav'n-ly king? A- wake the voice! A- wake the string!

2.   Now we will give him and bequeath
    This holly and this ivy wreath,
    To do him honour who's our King,
    And Lord of all this revelling.

Two verses of a poem from Robert Herrick's collection Hesperides *published in 1648. Herrick lived at Dean Prior near Buckfastleigh in Devon for many years and wrote a number of poems celebrating West Country customs and traditions.*

Evergreen Customs

Christmas Eve is traditionally the day for bringing holly and mistletoe into the house, as it was thought very unlucky to do so before. The tradition of taking greenery into the house goes back a long way. The Egyptians used branches of palm to celebrate the winter solstice, and the Romans used evergreen branches in their celebration of Saturnalia, when sacrifices were offered to protect winter-sown crops.

Holly is a male emblem, thought to bring fortune and fertility to the household, and protect against witches and the evil eye. In the west of England, girls used to decorate their beds with holly to ward off goblins. The number of berries is said to foretell winter weather, an abundance giving extra food for the birds in a harsh winter.

In the Midlands there was a tradition that if the first holly brought into the house at Christmas was prickly, then the master would rule for the coming year; but if the holly was smooth-leaved, then the mistress would rule.

Because of its clinging properties, ivy is the female counterpart to holly, and seen as a symbol of unpredictability. It is the sacred plant of Bacchus and believed to protect against drunkeness. The Holly Boy and Ivy Girl are still remembered in some places at Christmas.

The Holly and the ivy,
When they are both full grown,
Of all the trees that are in the wood,
The holly bears the crown:

The rising of the sun
And the running of the deer,
The playing of the merry organ,
Sweet singing in the choir . . .

Country writer Flora Thompson writes evocatively of both holly and ivy:

December and January are the bare months. Our grandmothers, when they compiled their floral calendar, could not find a flower for December at all and took the holly-berry instead. Their choice is understandable. Christmas and holly, holly and Christmas. Who could think of one without the other? But December has its own flower, the ivy, which they overlooked.

The ivy, even more than the holly, is Winter's own plant; for not only does it fruit, but it flowers also, between Michaelmas and Easter. Last of all native plants to flower, and first in the year to fruit, it provides a feast in a meagre time, first for the moths and bees, then for the birds. Right over Christmas, as long as the mealy pollen dust upon the flowers lasts, you will find upon any mild day a host of winged things of all sizes hovering and sipping at it, hurrying and buzzing and tumbling all the time as though they realised how short the day was and how certain the frost at the end of it.

The enemies of the ivy, woodmen, suburban gardeners and the like, greatly exaggerate its harmful influence upon whatever tree may happen to support it. The ivy, according to them, is a kind of vampire of the woods, taking the noble oak or elm into a deadly stranglehold and gradually crushing the life from it.

There is a tincture of truth in this belief. Upon light-limbed, scanty-foliaged trees, such as the birch or the mountain-ash, the growth of the ivy is always harmful, for it is a plant which loves light, and upon trees which do not give sufficient shade to keep it in check it will flourish only too well, and end by overtopping and destroying its unfortunate host. But upon the forest giant, oak or elm, or, more rarely, the beech, it will do no harm, but stand entwined like wedded king and queen, a joy to all beholders for centuries.

from *A Country Calendar and Peverel Papers*
FLORA THOMPSON

MISTLETOE

Mistletoe can be traced back to the Druids who believed it to have magic powers. They called it 'All Heal', as it could cure many diseases, promote fertility, avert bad luck, and protect homes from thunder and lightning. They considered the trees on which it grew to be sacred, and birds, like the mistle thrush, who visit and feed on the plants to be messengers from the gods. Mistletoe was celebrated in Norse mythology by Frigga the goddess of love and marriage; a kiss under the mistletoe symbolising her protection over the couple kissing. The English adopted this tradition two hundred years ago, but many country parsons still won't have it in decorations because of its association with the Druids.

At one time it was common throughout the apple orchards of the southern half of Britain, but now, with the sad decline in traditional apple trees, it mainly grows in the 'mistletoe triangle' of Herefordshire, Worcestershire, and Gloucestershire with the market at Tenbury Wells being the main supplier. Beware of French imports, they have fewer berries and are more spindly!

While holly and ivy was left till Twelfth Night, and in the old days till Candlemas Eve (1 February) mistletoe was often taken down at New Year's Eve. However in Worcestershire, to ensure good luck, a sprig was left till next New Year. Two mistletoe traditions have been noted in Staffordshire; farmer's wives would keep a bunch of mistletoe from one Christmas to the next to burn on the fire under the Christmas pudding; and also it was thought that a piece of mistletoe tied in a small bag and hung round the neck would safeguard against witchcraft.

Writing in the Cotswolds, Colin Howard has a particular mistletoe memory from the 1930s:

Old Corder was trying to sell me a bunch of mistletoe in the pub last night.

''Tes just what thee wants for thicky cottage o' thine,' he told me.

I didn't ask him what he meant by that.

'Right good mistletoe, this yere be,' he continued, holding it up and shaking it enticingly before me. 'Never failed yet, I do assure 'ee.'

'Why, has it been up somewhere already?' I asked.

He grinned.

'No, but every bit o' mistletoe do grow on a tree, don' 'um? And I do know the archard this yere bit come from.'

'I'm surprised at you, Mr. Corder!' said Mrs. Early. 'Fancy you knowing it, at your age!'

He grinned the wider, with the vanity of old age accused even in levity of amorous exploits.

'That archard 'a' seed a sight o' fun,' he said. 'Tes a wonder the trees did bear a single apple this year, the way them young things did shake the blossom off.'

The pub was looking very attractive last night, with a great fire rivalling the oil-lamp with its flickering flames, and holly stuck everywhere it would go, and gay paper-chains festooning the ceiling. There was Christmas in the air. The very beer seemed to taste more festive.

'Why don't you *give* the gennelman your mistletoe?' suggested Harry Woodman. *'Thee* don't need no mistletoe! Thee can do purty well wi'out, *I* know!'

'Aye, that I can, you!' answered old Corder complacently. 'A' right, sir, I'll give 'ee the mistletoe, and I do 'ope as it'll give thee a right 'appy Christmas.'

So, of course, I bought it from him, which gave rise to more jocularities, especially when I observed (meaning of course, that I had nowhere to hang it) that I shouldn't know what to do with it.

from *Cotswold Days*
Colin Howard

Mistletoe

Sitting under the mistletoe
(Pale green, fairy mistletoe)
One last candle burning low,
All the sleepy dancers gone,
Just one candle burning on,
Shadows lurking everywhere:
Someone came, and kissed me there.

Tired I was; my head would go
Nodding under the mistletoe
(Pale green, fairy mistletoe)
No footstep came, no voice, but only,
Just as I sat there, sleepy, lonely,
Stooped in the still and shadowy air,
Lips unseen – and kissed me there.

Walter de la Mare

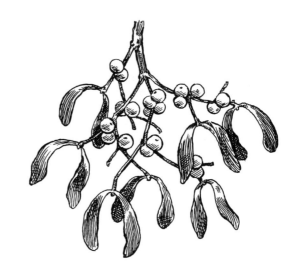

Magic Evergreens

Evergreens are believed to have magic powers: you must throw holly after runaway cattle to bring them back, or place a sprig in the cowshed to make them thrive. In Worcestershire farmers gave their Christmas mistletoe to the first cow to calve in the New Year, or put a little stolen hay in the Christmas Day feed to bring good luck to the farm. Ivy was saved from church Christmas decorations and fed to ewes to try and induce the conception of twin lambs.

The tradition of hanging wreaths of evergreens originated in Scandinavia; the round shape wards off wicked witches and evil spirits.

Other evergreens which were popular:
Rosemary – for remembrance and friendship.
Laurel – to protect, purify, and as a symbol of honour.
Bay – a symbol of power.
Yew – a defence against witches.
The Mistletoe Bough is steeped in tradition. It was a globe of evergreens looped with ribbons,

baubles and shiny red apples, and still being hung in some northern cottages in the 1970s. The Legend of the Mistletoe Bough is associated with several places including Minster Lovell in Oxon, and Marwell Hall at Owslebury in Hants.

CHRISTMAS TREES

A country Christmas would not be complete without a Christmas tree and its associations with family gatherings and the giving of presents. The very heart and centrepiece of the celebrations, it is full of ancient symbolism – evergreen is for survival, fire and light for the rebirth of the sun and everlasting life. Although its origins can be traced back to Egyptian, Greek and Roman customs, the tree as we know it first became popular in Alsace in Germany. One Christmas Eve Martin Luther is said to have been so moved by the sight of the star-lit sky through some fir trees, that he cut a tiny tree, hurried home, and decorated it with small candles to recreate the experience for his children. The custom was gradually brought to England in the late eighteenth century, and then popularised by Prince Albert in 1840.

In Devon, Cornwall and other areas the forerunner of the Christmas tree was 'The Kissing Bush'. This was a small furze bush dipped in water, and powdered with flour and studded with holly berries. It was not hung like the mistletoe, but planted in a decorated flower pot, and the custom was to 'kiss by the bush'.

THE YULE LOG

Before the advent of the Christmas tree, the bringing home of the Yule Log played a leading role in Christmas Eve traditions. Its pagan origins are from Northern Europe, where oak logs were lit in honour of the god Thor, and where Yule celebrations were to ensure the sun's survival and the return of warmth and light. The fire from the log was also believed to ward off evil spirits, and to warm the ancestral spirits who dwelt in the hearth.

The log was required to be given, 'found' or taken from your own property.

It was known as the 'Mock' in Cornwall, the 'Christmas Braund' in Dorset, the 'Brand' (pronounced 'Bron' or 'Brund') in Shropshire, and the Yule Clog in parts of Yorkshire. In Scotland the Yule Log was often a piece of birch stripped of its bark, and in the Highlands was identified with the 'Cailleach', or spirit of winter. In Ireland the log was known as the 'bloc na Nodlag', or Christmas block.

The log was dragged home in triumph from the woods, and anyone meeting the procession raised his hat in salute. In the hill-country of West Shropshire it was customary for horses to draw to the door a great trunk of seasoned oak, crab-apple tree, holly or yew. As soon as the log was brought in the Christmas Ale was tapped, and served to the men who had brought it in.

THE LIGHTING OF THE YULE LOG, ASHEN FAGGOTT OR HEARTH FIRE

The Yule Log had to rest on and be lit by the charred remains of last year's log. This ensured the continuity of good luck. It had to be lit at dusk and burn all night, and if possible kept alight for all twelve days of Christmas to bring good luck. Embers were raked up to it every night to carefully keep it alight.

KEEP THE FLAME

Words and Music: J. Coppin/J. Broomhall/M. Dolan ©

1. Now that the year's al-most o-ver, and
2. Now that the dark days are with you,
3. You have your whole life be-fore you, while

win-ter knocks hard on your door time to
now that the light's al-most gone and for
some just hang on to each day let's

hold out your hand to all those you can bring them
those far a-part from the place in your hearts keep the
set our sights high don't let that flame die, we'll

close to the fi-re once more

flame of your love burn-ing on So
fol-low the light all the way We'll

CHORUS

keep the flame burn – ing this Christ-mas

Let the light shine out so clear. Keep the flame burn-ing this

Christ – mas- time Keep the flame burn- ing all year.

Christmas is a time to keep the flame burning for love and friendship. This song is in the spirit of country christmasses past, present and future. It embraces the Winter Solstice and the Yule Log traditions, where fires are burned to symbolise the rebirth of the sun at the darkest time of the year – a celebration of the triumph of light over darkness.

Devon has the Ashen Faggott where nine bands of green ash are cut and bound together, and burned on an open fire. Unmarried girls would each choose a band, and the girl whose band burst first in the fire would be the first to marry. A fresh round of cider was drunk each time a band broke, as if they needed any excuse!

To conserve the good luck, certain people were not allowed to enter the room while the log was burning – for example no squinting person, and no flatfooted or barefooted women either!

The European tradition of the Yule Log was carried to North America. It still burns (1972) at Colonial Williamsburg, Virginia, and at the Empress Hotel, Victoria, British Columbia where, before Christmas dinner, a yule log is the centre of a procession by men in Elizabethan dress, and is lit with 'a splinter from a log of the bygone year'.

THE YULE CANDLE

In England a great candle used to either take the place of, or supplement the Yule log. It had to burn throughout the night and Christmas Day, or bad luck would come to the family the next year. They are still very popular in Scandinavia and Northern Europe.

In Devon and Somerset, The Yule Candle – which had to be a gift, often from the family's chandler, was lit by the master of the house, and burned through the night.

In Ireland, the Christmas candle is large, red and decorated with holly. It is set in a scooped-out turnip or vessel filled with bran, and placed in a main window to guide the Holy Family to shelter. Also in Ireland, only a woman named Mary may snuff out the candles on Christmas Day.

In Carmarthenshire, Wales there's still a tradition of fire-raising, with blazing torches carried through the streets, and in Yorkshire, grocers used to give their customers candles before the tradition of giving almanacs and calendars became widespread.

Canon Rawnsley was one of the founders of the National Trust, and a prolific writer on the natural history and customs of the Lake District. In this short extract from the late 1800s, he writes of 'Merrie Neets' and yule logs:

Christmastide time out of mind has been a time of great festivity. There is still a general feeling that work shall cease on Christmas Day and not be done save in a desultory manner until well into the New Year. The old custom of the 'Merrie Neet' has largely ceased to be. In old days one felt almost honour bound if one was a dalesman, to go off to the public-house of the vale as a guest at such a merry night . . . they were pleasant gatherings of friends when master and man and mistress and girl met on frank and open terms, and enjoyed a crack and a dance or a game of whist to their heart's content . . .

On the main hearth of the public-house, as indeed in the kitchens of most farmhouses, a yule-log was alight. I have spoken with old men who remember the taking into the farm kitchen of whole trees whose lighted end was on the hearth and once alight was not allowed to be extinguished until the tree had been consumed. In the little chapel of Newlands it was the duty of the clerk to see that such a yule-log was procured for Sunday use, and the log after having done duty at the service was handed out into the open and kept till the following Sunday called its services again into requisition . . .

from *Months at the Lakes*
REVD. H. D. RAWNSLEY

For some country folk, of course, nothing can ever match the old days. The depth of feeling this can arouse is wonderfully expressed in one of my favourite extracts from the work of John Moore:

Christmas, of course, is never what it was. We are reminded of this fact every year by old Jeremy Skinner, whose memory goes back seventy years or so and who sadly shakes his head as the landlord brings in the holly-sprigs to decorate his bar. 'In the old days,' says Jeremy, 'there was *real berries* on the holly, not just a little pip here and there. You could scarce see the leaves for red berries. That was because winters were harder then. Nature provided the berries as food for the birds.'

Always on Christmas Eve he pulls out of his pocket, and passes round the company in the bar, a very faded yellowing photograph in which he takes pleasure and pride. It represents a butcher's shop in the nearby town, and bears on its back the inscription, 'Christmas 1913'. If you look carefully – and Jeremy will insist that you do – you will make out, as it were through the mists of time, an array of enormous sides of beef, a dozen at least hanging from their hooks, with innumerable legs of mutton and loins of pork. Among them stands the proud butcher in his striped apron; at least Jeremy assures you it is the butcher, though his huge hands are like lumps of beef and his broad features peering between the haunches are liable to be confused with a boar's head.

'Look at it,' says Jeremy grimly. 'Just look. I simply ask you to look, that's all.'

We look.

'The rosettes,' says Jeremy, ' – You can just see 'em, up there in the left-hand corner – were worn by the prize-winning beasts at the Christmas Fat Stock Fair. Never bought anything but the best, he didn't. His sirloins would melt in your mouth. When I looked at my Christmas joint – if you call it a joint – this evening, and when I thought of those sirlons, well . . . believe it or not, but I minds the time when my old mother, and she was a hale and hearty woman, *couldn't lift down* our Christmas joint out of the larder; and "Jeremy," she called, "Jeremy me boy, just come here and give us a hand . . . "'

You would think, to listen to Jeremy, that Father Christmas had become a tattered beggar dressed in rags, that he who was once fat and prosperous and prodigal was now a pale starveling waif. And perhaps there would be some truth in this sad picture if the festival were simply a matter of beef and booze; instead of being a mood, a spirit, a leaven, something imponderable, a high wind blowing through our hearts. It is much more profound a mystery, fortunately, than the sirloins and the fat butcher in Jeremy's photograph; although even they are becoming a trifle mysterious as our memories fade and the photograph fades and the too too solid flesh melts into a peasoup fog.

'– There,' says Jeremy, pointing at the bottom left-hand corner with an old gnarled finger, 'that was snow.'

And indeed the photograph is flecked all over with white spots which we had thought were due to its great age.

'Snow,' repeats Jeremy firmly. 'When that photo was took, it was snowing. And it went on snowing for a week. None of your new-fangled green Christmases then! It showed for a week and, on Christmas day, after church, we sat in here at noon drinking our beer by candlelight. Why by candlelight? Because the drifts was above the winders of the bar, see. Drink our beer by candlelight we did, and when I say beer I mean beer, not this belly-chilling stuff we get today . . . '

from *The Season of the Year*
JOHN MOORE

FOOD AND DRINK CUSTOMS

Although feasting traditionally begins on Christmas Day, the eating of frumenty, Yule cakes, and huge Christmas Pies are all part of a country Christmas Eve.

CHRISTMAS PIES

Originally these were large and weighed over a hundredweight! They included meat, game, poultry, and wild birds. The custom was to cut them on Christmas Eve and serve as a standing dish throughout the Christmas season. Robert Herrick's poem is a reminder of a practice that died out around 1840:

> *Come guard the Christmas-pie,*
> *That the thief, though ne'er so sly,*
> *With his flesh-hooks don't come nigh,*
> *To catch it*
> *From him, who all alone sits there,*
> *Having his eyes still in his ear,*
> *And a deal of nightly fear,*
> *To watch it . . .*

Here's an eighteenth century Yorkshire recipe:

'Line a goodly pye dish with thick standing crust, and then bone a turkey, a goose, a partridge and a pigeon. Place the birds in the pye, so that the pigeon is inside the partridge, the partridge inside the goose, and the turkey covers the whole. Season well with pepper and salt, add spices, cover with butter, and seal with a lid – all save a little hole. Then, at the hole, blow into the dish a good blast of your breath, and suddenly stop the hole that your wind abide in the dish and raise up the crust, that it fall not adown.'

In west Cornwall, Mollie Bartlett remembers that Christmas Eve was celebrated with a supper of giblet pie and a special hot pork cake.

FRUMENTY

Thoughout Britain, frumenty or 'furmity' was eaten. This was milk boiled with barley or wheat and seasoned with spices. Richard Blakeborough in North Yorkshire in 1898 noted that it was always eaten at Christmas, and it was still being made as late as 1972 for his son from wheat prepared by a local miller descended from one who ground corn for the monks of Fountains Abbey. In Suffolk, it was the custom to put frumenty outside the door for the fairies.

POSSET

In Derbyshire the Christmas season began with the 'drinking of a posset'. This was a popular winter beverage consisting of hot milk, ale, eggs, treacle, ginger, nutmeg and other spices. It was a protection against colds, a cure for insomnia, and was even said to have cured a victim of the Eyam Plague after he narrowly escaped premature burial. Posset was served in specially designed pots, decorated and inscribed like loving-cups, with handles on both sides so that they could be passed easily among the family. It was eaten with one spoon passed from person to person.

YULE CAKES

In Yorkshire and Cumbria, sometimes frumenty was eaten with Yule cakes – heavy spiced buns, and with cheese. Yule cakes in Yorkshire were made of flour, yeast, raisins, currants, lemon peel and nutmeg. They were 3 inches thick, as large as dinner plates, and criss-crossed with a network of pastry. They were eaten with a slice from a large Wensleydale cheese upon which a cross had been scraped, while in Derbyshire the cakes were eaten with the Christmas sage cheese.

In the Scarborough area, a sort of parkin called 'pepper cake' or 'carol-singing cake' was made at Christmas: hence the rhyme

A little bit of pepper cake,
A little bit of cheese,
A cup of cold water
And a penny if you please.

Traditional Cumbrian buns at Christmas are 'Kendal wigs' and 'double sweaters', while in the Shrewsbury area, caraway buns dipped in ale were eaten on Christmas Eve.

In Somerset, the Christmas Eve festivities included hot cakes and nuts washed down with mulled ale, and in Cornwall at one time every housewife would make a small saffron or currant cake to give to each member of the family and each guest on Christmas Eve. The custom being for everyone to taste each other's cake as a mark of friendship.

Nuts were also eaten on Christmas Eve in Yorkshire, and if it was a full moon people went outside and said 'Yull, yull, yull my belly's full, cracking nuts and crying yull, yull, yull.' In the Lake District, this was sometimes called 'Nut-crack Night' because of the tradition of eating nuts cracked with the teeth!

In Warwickshire a large marrow, which had been decorated with ribbons and hung in the autumn, was stuffed and eaten at Christmas. At Penistone in South Yorkshire a large apple-pie would be made, and the whole family sat round the table eating it in turn using the same spoon in the same manner as the 'drinking of the posset'.

YULE BREAD

In Scotland this was baked between certain hours in the evening and signed with a cross. It was also thought lucky to keep a part of the Yule cake as long as possible.

WHITING CUSTOM IN KENT

At Folkstone the local fisherman chose eight of the best whiting out of every boat and sold them separately from the rest, and the profit paid for their annual Christmas Eve feast - 'A Rumbald'. The special fish were sold as 'Rumbald fish'.

Dickensian Festivals and Fairs are held in many places but Rochester in Kent, and Malton in Yorkshire may claim to be the oldest and best documented. Charles Dickens stayed at Easthorpe Hall near Malton and wrote much of 'A Christmas Carol' there, while Gadshill Place, near Rochester was his favourite Kentish home, and where he lived from 1856 until his death in 1870. In *The Pickwick Papers*, the action soon moves from London to Dickens' beloved Kent and to Manor Farm, the home of Mr Wardle:

They all repaired to the large kitchen, in which the family were by this time assembled, according to annual custom on Christmas Eve, observed by old Wardle's forefathers from time immemorial.

From the centre of the ceiling of this kitchen, old Wardle had just suspended with his own hands, a huge branch of mistletoe, and this same branch of mistletoe instantaneously gave rise to a scene of general and delightful struggling and confusion; in the midst of which, Mr Pickwick, with a gallantry that would have done honour to a descendant of Lady Tollimglower herself, took the old lady by the hand, led her beneath the mystic branch, and saluted her in all courtesy and decorum. The old lady submitted to this piece of practical politeness with all the dignity which befitted so important and serious a solemnity, but the younger ladies, not being so thoroughly imbued with a superstitious veneration for the custom; or imagining that the value of a salute is very much enhanced if it cost a little trouble to obtain it, screamed and struggled, and ran into corners, and threatened and remonstrated, and did everything but leave the room, until some of the less adventurous gentlemen were on the point of desisting, when they all at once found it useless to resist any longer, and submitted to be kissed with a good grace. Mr Winkle kissed the young lady with the black eyes, and Mr Snodgrass kissed Emily, and Mr Weller, not being particular about the form of being under the mistletoe, kissed Emma and the other female servants, just as he caught them. As to the poor relations, they kissed everybody, not even excepting the plainer portions of the young lady visitors, who, in their excessive confusion, ran right under the mistletoe, as soon as it was hung up, without knowing it! Wardle stood with his back to the fire, surveying the whole scene, with the utmost satisfaction; and the fat boy took the opportunity of appropriating to his own use, and summarily devouring, a particularly fine mince-pie, that had been carefully put by for somebody else.

Now, the screaming had subsided, and faces were in a glow, and curls in a tangle, and Mr Pickwick, after kissing the old lady as before mentioned, was standing under the mistletoe, looking with a very pleased countenance on all that was passing around him, when the young lady with the black eyes, after a little whispering with the other young ladies, made a sudden dart forward, and, putting her arm round Mr Pickwick's neck, saluted him affectionately on the left cheek; and before Mr Pickwick distinctly knew what was the matter, he was surrounded by the whole body, and kissed by every one of them.

It was a pleasant thing to see Mr Pickwick in the centre of the group, now pulled this way, and then that, and first kissed on the chin, and then on the nose, and then on the spectacles: and to hear the peals of laughter which were raised on every side; but it was a still more pleasant thing to see Mr Pickwick, blinded shortly afterwards with a silk handkerchief, falling up against the wall, and scrambling into corners, and going through all the mysteries of blind-man's buff, with the utmost relish for the game, until at last he caught one of the poor relations, and then

had to evade the blind-man himself, which he did with a nimbleness and agility that elicited the admiration and applause of all beholders. The poor relations caught the people who they thought would like it, and, when the game flagged, got caught themselves. When they were all tired of blind-man's buff, there was a great game at snap-dragon, and when fingers enough were burned with that, and all the raisins were gone, they sat down by the huge fire of blazing logs to a substantial supper, and a mighty bowl of wassail, something smaller than an ordinary wash-house copper, in which the hot apples were hissing and bubbling with a rich look, and a jolly sound, that were perfectly irresistible.

'This,' said Mr Pickwick, looking round him, 'this is, indeed, comfort.'

'Our invariable custom,' replied Mr Wardle. 'Everybody sits down with us on Christmas Eve, as you see them now – servants and all; and here we wait, until the clock strikes twelve, to usher Christmas in, and beguile the time with forfeits and old stories. Trundle, my boy, rake up the fire.'

Up flew the bright sparks in myriads as the logs were stirred. The deep red blaze sent forth a rich glow, that penetrated into the furthest corner of the room, and cast its cheerful tint on every face.

'Come,' said Wardle, 'a song – a Christmas song! I'll give you one, in default of a better.'
'Bravo!' said Mr Pickwick.

from *The Pickwick Papers*
CHARLES DICKENS

CAROL SINGERS AND WAITS

Nearly all villages, parishes and country towns had their own bands who performed in Church and at Wakes, Fairs and social occasions throughout the year. They became increasingly busy in the weeks before Christmas, but traditionally carol-singers and Waits made their rounds on Christmas Eve, and even sang right up until Christmas morning. This was recorded at Chaddleworth in Berkshire, and by Washington Irving on his visit to Yorkshire. It's not so surprising that they were known as 'Wakes' in East Yorkshire, while in the Scottish Highlands, groups of young boys who went round the houses chanting were known as '*gillean Nollaig*', 'Christmas lads', or *goisearan*, 'guisers'.

At Mallwyd in Gwynedd, North Wales, there is a 'Plygain' tradition of impromptu Welsh carol-singing during church services. At Padstow in Cornwall and in the Sheffield area there is still a strong tradition of carol-singing in the pubs before Christmas, with harmony parts being handed down through the generations.

In Somerset, 'Holly Riders' wore berry-wreathed hats and rode around hill-farms on Exmoor ponies singing carols for cakes, cider and money (of course) and in some Worcestershire villages, the Waits would go round at midnight wearing top hats and scarlet coats singing:

Arise, arise, make your mincepies.
A frosty night and a cold morning.

In the Yorkshire Dales, brass bands made their rounds on Christmas Eve:
'Once', said Mr T. Kilbride, a member of the Askrigg Band, 'we took the train to Aysgarth, played all up Bishopdale, lunched at Cray, then went up to Beckermonds. They hadn't had a band for fifteen years, and they made us all go inside and we played and played. They gave us frumenty. My! some of them bandsmen could eat. You could play well on frumenty. Then we walked over by Oughtershaw to Hawes, where by 9 pm we were met by two wagonettes which took us back to Askrigg.'

Wassailers went about villages during the Christmas holiday. They carried great wooden 'wassail bowls' decorated with evergreens and ribbons. This was originally filled with 'lamb's wool' – a drink made from hot ale, roasted crab apples, toast, nutmeg, sugar and eggs – but later on just ale or cider or whatever was offered!

In Yorkshire, wassaillers carried boxes with Advent images of Mary, Jesus, and the Three Kings among evergreens, and in Derbyshire, Nottinghamshire, and Lincolnshire, wassaillers carried a doll in a box surrounded by holly, apples, oranges and ribbons.

At Wensley and Winster in Derbyshire frightening figures with grotesque masks went round the houses demanding money 'without making the least effort to render any kind of hymn or carol'.

Traditional wassailling still occurred in the Truro area of Cornwall in 1970s, led by Harold Tozer.

GLOUCESTERSHIRE WASSAIL

Trad. arr. J. Coppin ©

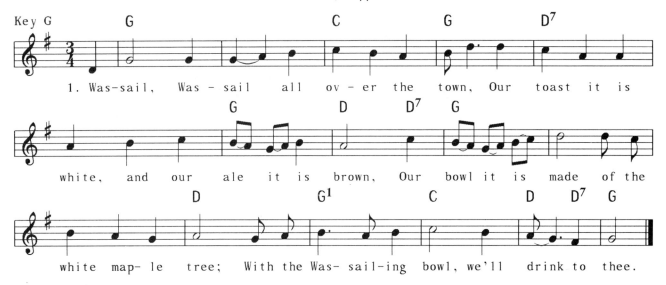

Key G

1. Was-sail, Was-sail all ov-er the town, Our toast it is white, and our ale it is brown, Our bowl it is made of the white map-le tree; With the Was-sail-ing bowl, we'll drink to thee.

2. So here is to Cherry and to his right cheek,
Pray God send our master a good piece of beef,
And a good piece of beef that may we all see;
With a wassailing bowl we'll drink to thee!

3. And here is to Dobbin and to his right eye,
Pray God send our master a good Christmas pie,
And a good Christmas pie that may we all see;
With our wassailing bowl we'll drink to thee!

CH. *Wassail, wassail, all over the town!*
Our toast it is white, and our ale it is brown,
Our bowl it is made of the white maple tree;
With the wassailing bowl we'll drink to thee!

4. So here is to Broad May and to her broad horn,
May God send our master a good crop of corn,
And a good crop corn that may we all see;
With the wassailing bowl we'll drink to thee!

5. And here is to Fillpail and to her left ear,
Pray God send our master a happy New Year,
And a happy New Year as e're he did see;
With our wassailing bowl we'll drink to thee!

CH. *Wassail, wassail, all over the town! etc.*

6. Come butler, come fill us a bowl of the best,
Then we hope that your soul in heaven may rest:
But if you do draw us a bowl of the small,
Then down shall go butler, bowl and all.

7. Then here's to the maid in the lily-white smock,
Who tripped to the door and slipped back the lock!
Who tripped to the door and pulled back the pin,
For to let these jolly wassailers in!

CH. *Wassail, wassail, all over the town! etc.*

One of the many versions of a traditional 'visiting' wassail known throughout Gloucestershire and Somerset. The verses were compiled by Ralph Vaughan Williams from various versions that he and Cecil Sharp heard at Buckland, Glos. and Little Sodbury near Bristol.

Gypsies also went round collecting money with their own special songs. This one is from the New Forest:

The roads are very dirty, my shoes are very thin,
I have a little pocket to put my money in.
Your pocket full of money, your cellar full of beer,
I wish you merry Christmas and happy New Year.

In the Cotswolds, the wonderful writer Laurie Lee remembers so vividly the time when he went 'carol-barking' in his beloved Slad Valley:

The week before Christmas, when snow seemed to lie thickest, was the moment for carol-singing; and when I think back to those nights it is to the crunch of snow and to the lights of the lanterns on it. Carol-singing in my village was a special tithe for the boys, the girls had little to do with it. Like hay-making, blackberrying, stone-clearing, and wishing-people-a-happy-Easter, it was one of our seasonal perks.

By instinct we knew just when to begin it; a day too soon and we should have been unwelcome, a day too late and we should have received lean looks from people whose bounty was already exhausted. When the true moment came, exactly balanced, we recognized it and were ready.

So as soon as the wood had been stacked in the oven to dry for the morning fire, we put on our scarves and went out through the streets, calling loudly between our hands, till the various boys who knew the signal ran out from their houses to join us.

One by one they came stumbling over the snow, swinging their lanterns around their heads, shouting and coughing horribly.

'Coming carol-barking then?'

We were the Church Choir, so no answer was necessary. For a year we had praised the Lord out of key, and as a reward for this service – on top of the Outing – we now had the right to visit all the big houses, to sing our carols and collect our tribute.

To work them all in meant a five-mile foot journey over wild and generally snowed-up country. So the first thing we did was to plan our route; a formality, as the route never changed. All the same, we blew on our fingers and argued; and then we chose our Leader. This was not binding, for we all fancied ourselves as Leaders, and he who started the night in that position usually trailed home with a bloody nose.

Eight of us set out that night. There was Sixpence the Tanner, who had never sung in his life (he just worked his mouth in church); the brothers Horace and Boney, who were always fighting everybody and always getting the worst of it; Clergy Green, the preaching maniac; Walt the bully, and my two brothers. As we went down the lane other boys, from other villages, were already about the hills, bawling 'Kingwenslush', and shouting through keyholes 'Knock on the knocker! Ring at the Bell! Give us a penny for singing so well!' They weren't an approved charity as we were, the Choir; but competition was in the air.

Our first call as usual was the house of the Squire, and we trouped nervously down his drive. For light we had candles in marmalade-jars suspended on loops of string, and they threw pale gleams on the towering snowdrifts that stood on each side of the drive. A blizzard was blowing, but we were well wrapped up, with Army puttees on our legs, woollen hats on our heads, and several scarves around our ears.

As we approached the Big House across its white silent lawns, we too grew respectfully silent. The lake near by was stiff and black, the waterfall frozen and still. We arranged ourselves shuffling around the big front door, then knocked and announced the Choir.

A maid bore the tidings of our arrival away into the echoing distances of the house, and while we waited we cleared our throats noisily. Then she came back, and the door was left ajar for us, and we were bidden to begin. We brought no music, the carols were in our heads. 'Let's give 'em "Wild Shepherds",' said Jack. We began in confusion, plunging into a wreckage of keys, of different words and tempo; but we gathered our strength; he who sang loudest took the rest of us with him, and the carol took shape if not sweetness.

This huge stone house, with its ivied walls, was always a mystery to us. What were those gables, those rooms and attics, those narrow windows veiled by the cedar trees. As we sang 'Wild Shepherds' we craned our necks, gaping into that lamplit hall which we had never entered; staring at the muskets and untenanted chairs, the great tapestries furred by dust – until suddenly, on the stairs, we saw the old Squire himself standing and listening with his head on one side.

He didn't move until we'd finished; then slowly he tottered towards us, dropped two coins in our box with a trembling hand, scratched his name in the book we carried, gave us each a long look with his moist blind eyes, then turned away in silence.

As though released from a spell, we took a few sedate steps, then broke into a run for the gate. We didn't stop till we were out of the grounds. Impatient, at last, to discover the extent of his bounty, we squatted by the cowsheds, held our lanterns over the book, and saw that he had written 'Two Shillings'. This was quite a good start. No one of any worth in the district would dare to give us less than the Squire.

So with money in the box, we pushed on up the valley, pouring scorn on each other's performance. Confident now, we began to consider our quality and whether one carol was not better suited to us than another. Horace, Walt said, shouldn't sing at all; his voice was beginning to break. Horace disputed this and there was a brief token battle – they fought as they walked, kicking up divots of snow, then they forgot it, and Horace still sang.

Steadily we worked through the length of the valley, going from house to house, visiting the lesser and the greater gentry – the farmers, the doctors, the merchants, the majors, and other exalted persons. It was freezing hard and blowing too; yet not for a moment did we feel the cold. The snow blew into our faces, into our eyes and mouths, soaked through our puttees, got into our boots, and dripped from our woollen caps. But we did not care. The collecting-box grew heavier, and the list of names in the book longer and more extravagant, each trying to outdo the other.

Mile after mile we went, fighting against the wind, falling into snowdrifts, and navigating by the lights of the houses. And yet we never saw our audience. We called at house after house; we sang in courtyards and porches, outside windows, or in the damp gloom of hallways; we heard voices from hidden rooms; we smelt rich clothes and strange hot food; we saw maids bearing in dishes or carrying away coffee-cups; we received nuts, cakes, figs, preserved ginger, dates, cough-drops, and money; but we never once saw our patrons. We sang as it were at the castle walls, and apart from the Squire, who had shown himself to prove that he was still alive, we never expected it otherwise.

As the night drew on there was trouble with Boney. 'Noël', for instance, had a rousing harmony which Boney persisted in singing, and singing flat. The others forbade him to sing it at all, and Boney said he would fight us. Picking himself up, he agreed we were right, then he disappeared altogether. He just turned away and walked into the snow and wouldn't answer when we called him back. Much later, as we reached a far point up the valley, somebody said 'Hark!' and we stopped to listen. Far away across the fields from the distant village came the sound of a frail voice singing, singing 'Noël', and singing it flat – it was Boney, branching out on his own.

We approached our last house high up on the hill, the place of Joseph the farmer. For him we had chosen a special carol, which was about the other Joseph, so that we always felt that singing it added a spicy cheek to the night. The last stretch of country to reach his farm was perhaps the most difficult of all. In these rough bare lanes,

open to all winds, sheep were buried and wagons lost. Huddled together, we tramped in one another's footsteps, powdered snow blew into our screwed-up eyes, the candles burnt low, some blew out altogether, and we talked loudly above the gale.

Crossing, at last, the frozen mill-stream – whose wheel in summer still turned a barren mechanism – we climbed up to Joseph's farm. Sheltered by trees, warm on its bed of snow, it seemed always to be like this. As always it was late; as always this was our final call. The snow had a fine crust upon it, and the old trees sparkled like tinsel.

We grouped ourselves round the farmhouse porch. The sky cleared, and broad streams of stars ran down over the valley and away to Wales. On Slad's white slopes, seen through the black sticks of its woods, some red lamps still burned in the windows.

Everything was quiet; everywhere there was the faint crackling silence of the winter night. We started singing, and we were all moved by the words and the sudden trueness of our voices. Pure, very clear, and breathless we sang:

> *As Joseph was a walking*
> *He heard an angel sing;*
> *'This night shall be the birth-time*
> *Of Christ the Heavenly King.*
>
> *He neither shall be bornèd*
> *In Housen nor in hall,*
> *Not in a place of paradise*
> *But in an ox's stall . . . '*

And two thousand Christmases became real to us then; the houses, the halls, the places of paradise had all been visited; the stars were bright to guide the Kings through the snow; and across the farmyard we could hear the beasts in their stalls. We were given roast apples and hot mince-pies, in our nostrils were spices like myrrh, and in our wooden box, as we headed back for the village, there were golden gifts for all.

from *Cider with Rosie*
LAURIE LEE

The Mellstock Band in *Under the Greenwood Tree* is very much based on memories of Thomas Hardy's father who was in one of the last of the village bands in Dorset. In this extract, it is late on Christmas Eve, and the band is about to go on their rounds:

Shortly after ten o'clock the singing-boys arrived at the tranter's house, which was invariably the place of meeting, and preparations were made for the start. The older men and musicians wore thick coats, with stiff perpendicular collars, and coloured handkerchiefs wound round and round the neck till the end came to hand, over all which they just showed their ears and noses, like people looking over a wall. The remainder, stalwart ruddy men and boys, were dressed mainly in snow-white smock-frocks, embroidered upon the shoulders and breasts in ornamental forms of hearts, diamonds, and zigzags. The cider-mug was emptied for the ninth time, the music-books were arranged, and the pieces finally decided upon. The boys in the meantime put the old horn-lanterns in order, cut candles into short lengths to fit the lanterns; and, a thin fleece of snow having fallen since the early part of the evening, those who had no leggings went to the stable and wound wisps of hay round their ankles to keep the insidious flakes from the interior of their boots . . .

Old William Dewy, with the violoncello, played the bass; his grandson Dick the treble violin; and Reuben and Michael Mail the tenor and second violins respectively. The singers consisted of four men and seven boys, upon whom devolved the task of carrying and attending to the lanterns, and holding the books open for the players. Directly music was the theme old William ever and instinctively came to the front . . .

'Times have changed from the times they used to be,' said Mail, regarding nobody can tell what interesting old panoramas with an inward eye, and letting his outward glance rest on the ground because it was as convenient a position as any. 'People don't care much about us now!

I've been thinking we must be almost the last left in the county of the old string players? Barrel-organs, and the things next door to 'em that you blow wi' your foot, have come in terribly of late years.'

'Ay!' said Bowman shaking his head; and old William on seeing him did the same thing.

'More's the pity,' replied another. 'Time was – long and merry ago now! – when not one of the varmits was to be heard of; but it served some of the quires right. They should have stuck to strings as we did, and kept out clarinets, and done away with serpents. If you'd thrive in musical religion, stick to strings, says I.'

'Strings be safe soul-lifters, as far as that do go,' said Mr Spinks.

'Yet there's worse things than serpents,' said Mr Penny. 'Old things pass away, 'tis true; but a serpent was a good old note: a deep rich note was the serpent.'

'Clar'nets, however, be bad at all times,' said Michael Mail. 'One Christmas – years agone now, years – I went the rounds wi' the Weatherbury quire. 'Twas a hard frosty night, and the keys of all the clar'nets froze – ah, they did freeze! – so that 'twas like drawing a cork every time a key was opened; and the players o' 'em had to go into a hedger-and-ditcher's chimley-corner, and thaw their clar'nets every now and then. An icicle o' spet hung down from the end of every man's clar'net a span long; and as to fingers – well, there, if ye'll believe me, we had no fingers at all, to our knowing.'

'I can well bring back to my mind,' said Mr Penny, 'what I said to poor Joseph Ryme (who took the treble part in Chalk-Newton Church for two-and-forty year) when they thought of having clar'nets there. "Joseph," I said says I, "depend upon't, if so be you have them tooting clar'nets you'll spoil the whole set-out. Clar'nets were not made for the service of the Lard; you can see it by looking at 'em," I said. And what came o't? Why, souls, the parson set up a barrel-organ on his own account within two years o' the time I spoke, and the old quire went to nothing.'

'As far as look is concerned,' said the tranter, 'I don't for my part see that a fiddle is much nearer heaven than a clar'net. 'Tis further off. There's always a rakish, scam-

PAST THREE A CLOCK

Words: Trad. G.R. Woodward/Music: Trad. arr. J. Coppin ©

Past three a clock, And a cold fros-ty morn - ing; Past three a
clock: Good morr-ow, mast-ers all. 1. Born is a ba - by, gen-tle as
may - be, Son of th' et - ern - al Fa - ther su - per - nal:

CH: *Past three a clock etc.*

2. Seraph choir singeth, angel bell ringeth:
   Hark how they rime it, time it and chime it.

CH: *Past three a clock etc.*

3. Myrrh from full coffer, incense they offer:
   Nor is the golden nugget witholden:

CH: *Past three a clock etc.*

4. Cheese from the dairy, bring they for Mary:
   And not for money, butter and honey:

CH: *Past three a clock etc.*

5. Thus they: I pray you, up, sirs, nor stay you
   Till ye confess him likewise, and bless him:

CH: *Past three a clock etc.*

I've enjoyed singing this old Waits carol for years. Both the tune 'London Waits' and the chorus words are traditional, while the verses were written by G.R. Woodward.

pish twist about a fiddle's looks that seems to say the Wicked One had a hand in making o'en; while angels be supposed to play clar'nets in heaven, or som'at like 'em if ye may believe picters.'

'Robert Penny, you was in the right,' broke in the eldest Dewy. 'They should ha' stuck to strings. Your brass-man is a rafting dog – well and good; your reed-man is a dab at stirring ye – well and good; your drum-man is a rare bowel-shaker – good again. But I don't care tho hears me say it, nothing will spak to your heart wi' the sweetness o' the man of strings!'

'Strings for ever!' said little Jimmy.

'Strings alone would have held their ground against all the newcomers in creation.' ('True, true!' said Bowman.) 'But clarinets was death.' ('Death they was!' said Mr Penny.) 'And harmonions,' William continued a louder voice, and getting excited by these signs of approval, 'harmonions and barrel-organs' ('Ah!' and groans from Spinks) 'be miserable – what shall I call 'em? – miserable –'

'Sinners,' suggested Jimmy, who made large strides like the men and did not lag behind with the other little boys.

'Miserable dumbledores!'

'Right, William, and so they be – miserable dumbledores!' said the choir with unanimity.

from Under the Greenwood Tree
Thomas Hardy

In her novel *The Golden Arrow*, Shropshire author Mary Webb writes evocatively of the time the 'Slepe' (or Ratlinghope) handbell ringers came to call:

Faint tinklings – quick and small as a robin's 'chink-chink' – came up the dark slopes above Slepe on Christmas evening. The handbell ringers were coming Christmassing, as they did every year when the weather allowed them.

Joe and Lily had just arrived, and they were all having tea, Deborah apart in an armchair by the fire, withdrawn in heavy unconsciousness. She had got up at John's entreaty. It had taken her hours to dress – so hard was it to fix her attention on anything – and, once downstairs, she sank again into stupor . . .

'It's the Slepe handbells!' cried Lily. 'What a treat!' Handbells, and such festivities, had never come to Bitterley.

Joe welcomed the diversion. 'Aye, there they come,' he said, 'Cadwallader an' all.'

'Damn who?' said Deborah.

'Best say summat, Joe,' murmured John anxiously.

'Cadwallader, Deb', said Joe. 'Damn Cadwallader and his missus and his kid,' he repeated, with great relief at having found a lamb for the sacrifice.

Deborah went back into her stillness.

The gate clicked and John went to the door.

'Well, neighbours!' he said, 'you're kindly welcome. What'm you going to give us?'

The postmaster, as head of the band, and bass bell, said he'd thought of 'Ox and ass,' which every one knew to mean 'Good Christian men, rejoice'; though why the ringers always named it after a line in the second verse, no one asked.

'And a very suitable 'un,' said Mrs Arden, 'for if we 'anna got an ox we'n two cows, and our Joe's an ass if ever there was one.'

When the merriment subsided they grouped themselves in a semicircle, Job Cadwallader having been urgently entreated to come in at the right moment and not half a note too late as he always did; the postmaster cleared his throat and said in the tone of one inciting a mob to evil-doing –

'The chime.'

Obediently, under the large stars on their black velvet, the chime of eight bells rippled out – with one dotted note occasioned by Job.

'You did it agen!' said the postmaster, in a grieved voice.

'I did me best,' said Job; 'but when I'm expecting 'im to waggle he dunna, and as soon as I've giv up expecting he does it sudden-like.'

'You're not master of your bell,' said Shakeshaft solemnly.

'Ca'waller ain't mas'er of his missus nor hisself, so it ain't likely he'd be master of anythink as determined as a bell,' said the blacksmith, who had taken a good deal of refreshment.

'If you'm Christmas peart when you'm only done the Parson's and the Squire's and two more, what'll you be when we'm through?' asked the postmaster.

The blacksmith subsided.

'Now! The chime again and into the hymn right off.'

The antique tune, sweetly and emphatically uttered by the bells, slipped out over the great plateau, pearl-tinted in the light of stars and the rising moon. The sense of the words was in the air – they were so well known by all – and they brought the strange joy with which some old Christian hymns touch the human heart, a joy alien to those here – and to most human beings – who are pagan at the core.

Even John's Christianity was earthy, fuller flavoured than any formulated creed can be – but perhaps not fuller flavoured or as natural or as rich as the Gospel story, if we knew it in its entirety. This was John's favourite carol because it brought in the animal world.

'Ox and ass before Him bow.'

'Aye!' he murmured; 'the dumb things know.'

Mrs Arden tapped her foot to the tune and found no trial of faith in the words; for every birth to her was wondrous, and she was only a little less thrilled by the coming of this marvel two thousand years ago than by the coming of a neighbour's child to-night.

Lily rocked idly in the old rocking-chair. If her rather vague and muddled ideas could have been unravelled they would have resolved themselves into a kind of pity for a woman who had the pains of maternity without the ameliorations of wifehood.

Joe sat contentedly drinking in the picture of childhood and cattle and mangers; for these were things he knew, friendly and homely. But there was not in him or in any of those present the sense of sinfulness implied in the carol – for that sense is an artificial product of civilization, and though it may be both beautiful and necessary in some environments it is not so among simple people living normal lives.

'What a dot-an'-go-one chap you are, Job,' said the postmaster. 'What ails you, hopping on the note like that?'

'I done my best,' said Job. 'I fixed my eye on the clapper three bells afore my note, and I puts me tongue out and I thought I should catchen 'im, but I didna. Belike I will some time.'

'When bit-bats sleep yeads up'ard and women sleep alone,' piped a small man who rang the treble bell. He was dapper as a robin, and wore a perpetual smile, as if he had thought of a splendid joke in babyhood, and had never yet told it. He was the wit of the party; there was much mirth and covering of large mouths with large hands at his remarks.

'Will!' said the tenor bell, who was parish clerk; 'such speaking's not convenient.'

'Nor yet sleeping alone bain't!' said the blacksmith, who had an enormous voice, which gave to his remarks (all broad in humour) a kind of shamelessness.

'Now, now,' said the postmaster, finding his flock rather unruly; 'manners afore ladies, men! We'll play "As Joseph was a'walking."'

Afterwards John asked for "Lead, kindly Light," with a sorrowful glance at the silent figure by the fire.

'Oh! laws me!' said Patty, 'that gloomy thing agen! What a man! What do we want wi' encircling gloom and angels' faces, when we'm just going to sit down to Christmas beef an' pickle?'

'And beer,' said the blacksmith, outside, in tones that would have been persuasive if they had not been stentorian.

'Ringing first,' said the leader firmly . . .

'Well, thank you kindly!' said John at the end. 'And now come you all in, and have a drop and some pies.'

from *The Golden Arrow*
MARY WEBB

Over the Snows

Words: Margiad Evans/Music: J.Coppin ©

1. You do not go where the lark is high but you find your-self un-der that part of the sky where he is sing-ing

2. You do not look for the wind where it blows through the stems of the iv-y woods ov - er the snows, but you find your face pressed a-gainst its breast where the cold storm is wing-ing.

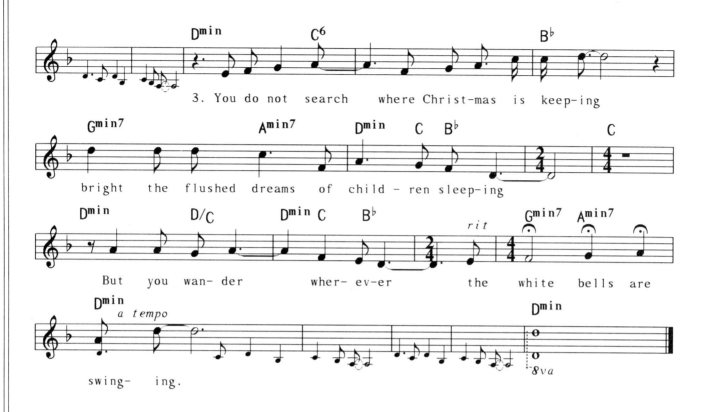

3. You do not search where Christ-mas is keep-ing
bright the flushed dreams of child-ren sleep-ing
But you wan-der wher-ev-er the white bells are
swing- ing.

A setting of a wonderfully atmospheric poem by Margiad Evans, who lived for much of her life near Ross-on-Wye in Herefordshire. Originally entitled 'Christmas Song', the poem is taken from her book A Candle Ahead *published in 1956.*

Animal Traditions and Folklore

The Midwinter rituals of dressing up as horses and horned animals are of pagan origin and fairly widespread throughout Britain. They are believed to ward off evil spirits, and in customs where they are 'killed' and reborn, thought to represent the dying year, and the rising of the new year.

The Kent 'Hoodening' custom at Hythe features a wooden horse, hand-bell ringers, carol singers and morris dancers, and survived at Wal-mer and Deal till early this century. In recent years it has been revived at Whitstable, Folkestone, and Tonbridge.

The 'Mari Lwyd' (The Grey Mare) has survived at Llangynwyd and Pencoed, Mid-Glamorgan. This was once a well-known custom in South Wales. A decorated horse's head is carried from house to house accompanied by singing, dancing, food, drink, and battles recited in Welsh verse.

In Yorkshire and Lancashire 'the old horse'

used to go round with the mummers, while Castleton in Derbyshire and the Sheffield area has 'the old tup' tradition. A sheep's head surmounts a sack worn by a man, and his attendants include a 'butcher', a 'woman', and an 'old man', who pretends to collect the blood in a basin.

At Stourton in Wiltshire was 'The Christmas Bull' as witnessed by E. E. Balch in 1908:
'Quite distinct from the mummers, though also coming on Christmas Eve, was the Christmas bull. The head of a bull with great bottle eyes, large horns, and lolling tongue, was manipulated by a man stooping inside a body composed of a broomstick, a hide of sacking and a rope tail. The bull knocked at the door with its horns, and, if allowed to enter, chased the young people round the house, with fearsome curvets and bellowings. Even in the surrounding parishes the Christmas bull is unknown, and I have never heard of the custom being practised in other parts of the country. The man in whose possession the bull was until quite recently, knows that it has been in his family for over one hundred years. It was used till about ten years ago.'

However this unusual custom was not unique to Wiltshire as it was also known in Dorset and at Kingscote in Gloucestershire.

On Christmas Eve cattle and other livestock were given an extra supply of food. In Scotland, Cumberland and much of Britain every horse and cow had its 'Christmas sheaf' in its stall, sheaves of corn were spread out in the fields for the sheep, and in Cheshire hens were given double rations of grain.

At midnight bees are said to hum the 100th Psalm in their hives – while in the Highlands of Scotland bees are believed to leave their hives at three o'clock on Christmas morning only to return again immediately.

LEGEND OF THE OXEN AND CATTLE KNEELING

Cattle and oxen are believed to drop to their knees in adoration at midnight, though many farmers still adhere to the old calendar, and believe it occurs on 5 January, Old Christmas Eve. Here's the Rev. Francis Kilvert's moving account from Herefordshire in 1878:

Speaking of the blowing of the Holy Thorn and the kneeling and weeping of the oxen in old Christmas Eve (to-night) Priscilla said, 'I have known old James Meredith 40 years and I have never known him far from the truth, and I said to him one day, "James, tell me the truth, did you ever see the oxen kneel on old Christmas Eve at the Weston?" And he said, "No, I never saw them kneel at the Weston but when I was at Hinton at Staunton-on-Wye I saw them. I was watching them on old Christmas Eve and at 12 o'clock the oxen that were standing knelt down upon their knees and those that were lying down rose up on their knees and there they stayed kneeling and moaning, the tears running down their faces."'

In some places cattle were even believed to acquire the gift of speech on Christmas Eve, but it was considered dangerous for any human to listen to their talk. Whoever did so was thought to meet with misfortune or to even hear the cattle speaking of his own death.

In Cornwall, sheep are thought to turn to the east and bow their heads in memory of the sheep belonging to the shepherds at Bethlehem.

THE OXEN

Words: Thomas Hardy/Music: J. Coppin ©

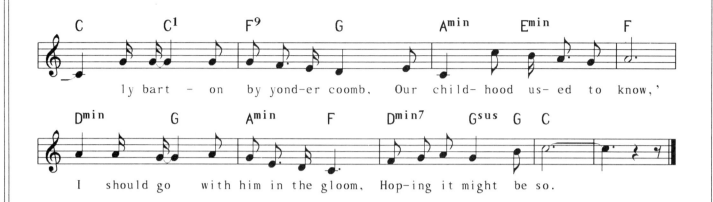

ly bart - on by yond-er coomb, Our child- hood us- ed to know,'
I should go with him in the gloom, Hop-ing it might be so.

One of Thomas Hardy's most popular Christmas poems first published in 1917. Inspired by the legend that on Christmas Eve, it is said, cattle pay their own tribute to the nativity by dropping to their knees in an attitude of devotion.

Other Folklore Traditions

Foretelling the Future

Girls who want to see an image of their future partner should walk backwards around the nearest pear tree nine times, while a superstition from Devon for unmarried girls was recorded by Sarah Hewett in 1900 – 'An unmarried girl who desires to learn something of her prospects in marriage goes to the door of the fowlhouse on Christmas Eve, and taps it smartly. If a hen first cackles, the girl's future is not encouraging, but if a cock crows first, the girl, it was believed, would be married before the end of the year.' If a cock did crow first, it doesn't leave much time!

In Northamptonshire, the girl who goes into the garden at midnight and plucks twelve sage leaves, will see the shadowy form of her future husband approaching from the opposite end of the garden. In Oxfordshire a dumb or dough cake is made in silence by a girl. The cake is placed on the hearth, and she pricks her initials on the cake. Then, leaving the door open, she must wait in silence until the clock strikes midnight, when her future husband should walk into the room, prick his initials on the cake, and then walk out again.

Bell-ringing to welcome in Christmas was widespread at one time, and at Ruardean in Gloucestershire, an Elizabethan benefactor left 5 shillings for the ringing of a 2 hour 'virgin peal' to welcome in Christmas. In Lancashire and Cheshire it is believed 'the bells of churches buried by earthquakes may be heard to ring.'

There was a widely held belief that ghosts never appear on Christmas Eve. All ghosts, witches and evil creatures of the night had their powers sus-

pended – 'No fairy takes, nor witch hath power to charm – So hallowed and so gracious is the time.' (from *Hamlet*.) However one exception is the ghost of the Egremont pony rider in Cumbria:

What is Christmas without a ghost? For in the Tarpot district of Egremont a ghost only appears on Christmas Eve. Legend has it that way back in the middle ages a fell farmer left an Egremont tavern on a stormy Christmas Eve to ride his pony back to his lonely farmhouse where he lived alone. Having imbibed to his full capacity, he was given a rousing send-off by his friends – and neither he nor his pony was ever seen again. Certain Egremont people place great credence in the legend, and claim that their parents or grandparents have actually 'seen' the ghostly rider on his pony on Christmas Eve.

from *Lakeland Ghosts*
Gerald Findler

The Irish believed that the gates of Paradise opened on the hour of midnight, and if anyone died at this time they would go straight up to heaven.

In Cornwall and the Black Country it is said that on Christmas Eve the fairies meet at the bottom of the mine and perform a mass in celebration of the birth of Christ, as in the Legend of the Giant and Spriggans of Trencrom mine:

It was from the top of Trencrom Hill, near St Ives, that the Trencrom or Trecobben Giant used to play his game of 'bob button' with the giant of St Michael's Mount. The Mount can be seen plainly from the top of Trencrom Hill.

The boulders that Cormoran of St Michael's Mount threw back are strewn all over the hillside to this day. But before he died, it is said that the giant of Trencrom buried a massive treasure of gold deep in the heart of the hill.

Perhaps that is why the spriggans came to Trencrom. The spriggans were a race of fairy warriors, said by some to be appallingly ugly and by others to be extremely beautiful and able to change shape at will. They were the guardians of the ancient places – the old forts, stone castles and circles – and the treasure within them. They were also said to be able to bring down storms and, like the piskies, would take away human children and leave changelings of their own.

Yet some of the miners believed that they were basically a good people, and the old men would say if you went down the deepest mines at midnight on Christmas Eve you would hear them celebrating midnight mass, singing 'Now well, now well' – 'Noël, Noël' – in sweet, clear voices to the music of a mighty organ rumbling under the rock.

from *When I set out for Lyonesse*
JUDITH COOK

Very few people now experience a white Christmas, but country writer Ian Niall has a special childhood memory of being snowed in at Christmas in Scotland:

It didn't happen overnight, and I remember things that led up to our being snow-bound more clearly than the day when the snow fell in earnest. I was about five years old and my impressions are those of a child fascinated by the sight of the pump beyond the kitchen window wearing a sort of overcoat with straw stuffing, the trough from which the plough horses drank brimming over in a lip of thick ice, and away beyond our march boundary, and the round hills of our neighbours' land, the Galloway hills, glazed with snow that was sometimes dazzling. Before the snow came, all sorts of precautions were taken. Swedes were piled in places where they could be easily fed to cattle, straw was put down at one of the gates, sheep were herded into the stackyard. It was only a few days until Christmas when we heard stories of trains being stuck.

I was coddled and swathed in scarves and extra woollen garments before I was taken up through the court to

see how icicles had formed on the gates. The stable barrow was firmly fixed in the midden, which was as hard as iron. It was coming again, the year of the big snow, someone said. The frost was getting at potatoes in the barn and wild birds were tame, or so hungry that they could be caught without difficulty. The peat stack and the coal heap were welded, and it was necessary to break the fuel out. The milk churn lids were sticking to a man's fingers. It only needed a fall of snow, and we should be wrapped up in a blanket, cut off from the outside world.

There were snow buntings in the stackyard, and a sort of steam was rising from the shed where calves and bullocks were penned: a wall of humid air against the barrier of freezing atmosphere outside. I remember being hurried out to the door to watch the geese coming. It was long past the time for the geese to come. They had been with us for two or three months, but now a fresh wave of geese came out of the north. There was snow on the way, they said, and it was a good thing we had hams hanging, oatmeal and flour, tea and sugar by the sack.

It snowed in the night. No one told me. I looked at the skylight. Every morning I had admired the frost pictures on the glass, but now the attic bedroom was dimly lit. A covering of snow made the ceiling look yellow. It had never looked yellow before.

When I got down to the kitchen, the windows were steamed on the inside but the steam was freezing on the window ledge. The glare of snow beyond the windows stretched upwards to the sky and hills, and fields were blended with far-off higher hills and the heavens above them. It snowed all day, and late in the afternoon a path was cut across to the byre and the dairy and then another path to the stable, the cartshed and the open-sided shed where bullocks bellowed and hung their heads over the spruce poles dribbling straw on to the snow. By the next day we were cut off. It was harder to free the pump handle than it had been. Two kettles of water were needed and the water running over the spout of the pump began to turn into a stick of ice.

Everything became capped with snow. The drystone walls disappeared and indoors the few newspapers became tattered and torn, they were read so often. No one

had ever had so much time on their hands before, I think. There was nothing to do but talk, drink the hot gruel that was made to warm the body up before an excursion was made to feed the standing-in beasts. The first day's milk was put in churns, the second day's supply went into spare churns and scalded butts, and then the pigs and calves began to get double rations. We had come to a crisis, it seemed, although I was hardly old enough to understand just how serious it was. Someone was sent out over the fields to make contact with the nearest cottage. The journey might have taken half an hour, but it wasn't until nightfall that word came back that everyone else was in the same predicament. The roads were closed. I forget whether anyone said that it was Christmas Eve or Christmas Day. I remember there was a serious attempt to dig a path across country so that milk might be sledged out on a hay sledge, but perhaps the creamery itself was isolated or the horsepower for such an enterprise couldn't be managed on ground that crossed covered-in burns and waterholes.

I enjoyed the company, the warmth of over-large peat fires and the feeling of being secure in a closed-in world. The snow began to melt after some days. It revealed the line of drystone dikes and black ditches, gaunt thorn trees and stunted bushes one day, and the next the road was running in slush. Someone found a ewe huddled in between a wall and the melting mound of a snowdrift. I remember being taken to see the miracle of how that sheep had survived and noticing the stained ground on which she had lain. As far as I can remember we lost no stock. The milk fattened the pigs, but of course gallons of it had to be poured away.

It seemed a lot colder when it was all over, and bleak too. The wind moaned in the porch and the porch roof leaked where the melting snow seeped in. Such a thing never happened again for me to remember it. I suppose you might say that was one Christmas we never had, for no one took note that it had come or remarked upon it until it had gone.

from *Country Matters*
IAN NIALL

CHRISTMAS EVE

Words: John Drinkwater/Music: J. Coppin ©

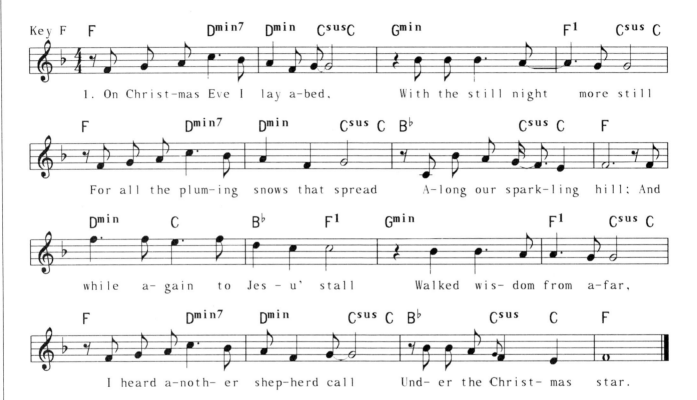

1. On Christ-mas Eve I lay a-bed, With the still night more still For all the plum-ing snows that spread A-long our spark-ling hill: And while a-gain to Jes-u' stall Walked wis-dom from a-far, I heard a-noth-er shep-herd call Und-er the Christ-mas star.

2. Along the lane his carol came,
   But not of Bethlehem,
   A burning boy, he knew a flame
   But not the flame of them:
   'This Christmas Eve from courting home
   I am a bachelor,
   But soon the snows again will come,
   And I'll be wed before.'

3. All one with kings from Bible-page,
   And holy shepherds old,
   Went yeoman love in pilgrimage
   Across the Christmas wold.
   'Goodwill,' he sang, 'Goodwill, Goodwill,'
   Or seemed to me to sing,
   While some glad girl beyond the hill
   Dreamt of a new-born king.

A Cotswold carol written by John Drinkwater just after the First World War. As one of the Dymock Poets (along with Rupert Brooke, Edward Thomas, Robert Frost and others) he was a frequent visitor to Gloucestershire, and lived for a time in the Cotswolds.

CHRISTMAS DAY

'At Christmas be merry and thankful withal,
And feast thy poor neighbours, the great with the small'

Thomas Tusser, sixteenth century

HIGH IN THE HEAVEN

Words: Charles Causley/Music: J. Coppin ©

2. Silver the frost
   It shines on the stem.
   As we now journey
   To Bethlehem.

3. White is the ice
   At our feet as we tread,
   Pointing a path
   To the manger-bed.

4. High in the Heaven
   A gold star burns
   Lighting our way
   As the great world turns.

A setting of a Charles Causley poem full of wonderful imagery.

CHRISTMAS DAY

The Anglo-Saxon tradition is that Christmas Day is the most important of the season and always spent at home with the family. It starts with stockings and presents from Father Christmas, and then family presents are taken from under the Tree and opened before or after church service. This is followed by a Christmas dinner of roast turkey or goose and all the trimmings, then a flaming plum pudding, cracker-pulling, paper hats, port, Stilton, nuts and chocolate for the children. After this might come games, a walk, then ghost stories and singing in the evening.

The excitement and anticipation of opening presents on Christmas morning is wonderfully captured in this much requested extract from Winifred Foley's *A Child in the Forest*:

'THE DOLL'

If the chapel treat was the highlight of our life in summer, Christmas was the pinnacle of our winter delight, though most of the joy was in the anticipation. Every year for many years I spent weeks getting excited about a hopeless dream. I wanted – oh how I wanted – a doll. I knew it was quite impossible for Mam and Dad to buy me one. I had no luck praying for one, and it wasn't any good asking Dad to put a word in for me in that quarter, because I'd heard him and his butties argue and come to the conclusion that there couldn't be a God, or at any rate not one who worried about us as individuals.

But Father Christmas was quite a likely benefactor, though he too had his limitations. *My* dad had explained to me that as Father Christmas was such an old man, with his long white beard, he couldn't be expected to carry big things for all the children. I should have to wait my turn for a doll. Meantime I must be satisfied with something small, like a penny box of beads, and an orange if I was lucky. My turn for a doll seemed a long time coming.

My patience ran out one autumn when I was nine years old. Gladys, my best friend, who already had a nice doll, was given the most fantastic doll you ever saw. I didn't begrudge Gladys anything – she let me nurse her doll, and dress and undress it. But that was like being a nanny, not the same as having your own baby. The new doll was the size of a child, had long hair, eyes that opened and shut, and wore socks and shoes. Gladys's dad had won it at Barton fair. The doll was much too grand to play with, and was put on display in their cottage. All the village children, and quite a few grown-ups, called at Gladys's home for the privilege of seeing it.

As far as I was concerned, matters regarding a doll had now come to a head. I couldn't help Father Christmas's decrepitude – he would *have* to bring me a doll this Christmas. I gave him plenty of warning by shouting my request up the chimney weeks in advance of the usual time. Towards Christmas I started to write notes to him as well, with a stub of pencil given me by a neighbour as payment for running errands.

I was puzzling out how best to put my case to him with the limited spelling and vocabulary of a nine-year-old, when Dad came in. I told him I was making a bargain with Father Christmas: providing he brought me a doll this time, he needn't bring me anything else ever. But it had to be a doll big enough to sit on my lap, and have hair, and eyes that opened and shut.

'I be a'feared 'tis no good thee exing Feyther Christmas for that sart o' doll, my wench. 'Im do only take that sart to the rich people's young uns,' Dad warned me kindly.

'You do want to tell the silly old bugger off then. Tell 'im they rich people can afford to buy dolls for their children. It's the likes o' we lot 'im do want to bring the best toys to. Why ever 'aven't 'im got more sense than that?'

Father, who usually had an explanation for everything under the sun, scratched his head and admitted himself 'proper flummoxed'.

Bess said I'd be lucky to get anything if Father Christmas overheard me calling him a silly old bugger. Just because she was gone thirteen years old, and would soon be going into domestic service, she fancied herself too grown up to ask Father Christmas for anything. Anyway, then she would be rich enough to buy anything she wanted, for my auntie in Bristol was getting her a job with the fantastic wage of five shillings a week.

With hope only slightly diminished, I continued to shout my order up the chimney, and to send up my notes when the draught was strong enough to stop them falling back into the fire.

My little brother fell asleep on Christmas Eve long before I did. I kept poking him awake to keep me company, but it was no good. I must have been awake for hours, when I heard stealthy footsteps coming up the stairs. It must be Father Christmas! Should I look, or shouldn't I? I had the patchwork quilt pulled right up to my eyes – he wouldn't notice, if I just took a peep. I suddenly felt terrified.

It was a bit of an anticlimax when I saw my sister in the doorway! 'Oh gawd! I thought you was Feyther Christmas!' It seemed to me that she was hiding something behind her back.

'If thee doosn't go to sleep Feyther Christmas wunt come at all,' she scolded me.

'I can't,' I wailed, 'thee'lt 'a' to 'it I over the yud wi' the coal 'ammer.'

I banged my obstinate head into the bolster. 'Go to sleep, you silly little bitch,' I told myself crossly.

It was my excited little brother who poked *me* awake in the morning. 'Look – Feyther Christmas a' brought I a tin whistle, a orange, a bag o' marbles an' some sweets.'

I sat bolt upright, like a Jack-in-the-Box. My doll, my doll! Had Father Christmas brought my doll?

At the bottom of my piece of the bed was propped the ugliest apology for a doll one could ever hope not to see.

It looked for all the world like an old, darned, black woollen stocking, lumpily stuffed, with a bit of old ribbon tied tightly round the foot to form its head. The eyes were two odd-sized buttons, and it grimaced from ear to ear with a red woollen gash of a mouth.

After all that cajoling up the chimney, after all the notes I'd written, fancy him bringing me a thing like that! He must think me a horrible little girl to treat me so, but I couldn't be that horrible! Mam came in, looking a bit anxious, but she said, bright enough, 'Well then, Feyther

Christmas didn't forget. 'Im did bring a doll for you.'

'Yes, an' 'im can 'ave the bugger back.'

Mother looked crestfallen. 'It won't break, like one o' they china dolls.'

'It's ugly, an' boss-eyed, an' got no 'air, and 'ow would you like it if the angels sent you a babby as ugly as *that*?'

Then I pulled the quilt over my head, to show I had cut myself off from the season of goodwill, and everyone concerned with it.

But Mam hadn't. After a bit she came back and sat on the bed. She didn't say anything, and my curiosity soon overcame me enough to have a peep at what she was up to.

Her baby boy, born a year after my little brother, had died; I thought he'd gone to heaven to be pampered and fussed over by the angels. Mam had kept a few of his baby clothes, though in general the women in our part of the village pooled their baby clothes to help each other out. Now she was dressing my doll up in a flannel nightdress, a bonnet and a piece of shawl. Held up in Mam's arms and cuddled against her neck, it looked like a real infant from the back. I was tempted to be won round. Mam left it, all snugly wrapped up, on the bed, while she went to get breakfast.

I and the doll were soon downstairs with the rest of the family, sitting at the table. Mam was in a specially good humour with me. We didn't have such things as bacon and eggs even on Christmas Day, but as a great treat old Auntie had given us half a tin of Nestlé's milk to share out on our toast. As if that were not enough, she'd given us each a shiny new penny as well. I felt warmed and loved again. I made a bit of sop in a saucer, with a drop of my tea and a bit of the bread and milk, and pretended to spoon it into my doll's mouth, before taking her out.

I knew that other children might laugh at her ugliness as they did at Lil Wills's poor little looney sister, so I decided to take her for a walk on my own. Miss Phillips, whose cottage garden adjoined ours, was just coming back from the ashmix with an empty bucket.

'My, my, Polly!' It looks as though Feyther Christmas 'a' brought you a real big doll this time. Let me 'ave a look at 'er.'

I loved the inside of Miss Phillips' neat, tidy cottage, but none of us were much taken with her – she nagged us for playing noisily, and wouldn't let us play ball where we wanted to. I gave her one of my ferocious scowls to put her off, but she insisted on following me and unwrapping the piece of shawl to see what I'd got.

'Oh, my gawd, that'un 'ould do better to frighten the birds off the gyarden. I reckon Feyther Christmas musta took 'im from a crow's nest.'

How dare she? I bridled like an insulted mother! I doubled my scowl, and threw in my monkey face for good measure.

'Never mind,' I said to the doll, when we were out of earshot. ''Er's a nasty old bisom, and your mammy 'ouldn't change you for all the money in the world.'

Miss Phillips' insults cemented my feeling for my new charge. From then, she became the object of my affection.

from *A Child in the Forest*
WINIFRED FOLEY

While staying at Chigwell in Essex, Charles Dickens witnessed one of the earliest Christmas trees in Britain. In this piece he describes with wonder and amazement what must have been one of the most heavily laden trees ever:

I have been looking on, this evening, at a merry company of children assembled round that pretty German toy, a Christmas tree. The tree was planted in the middle of a great round table, and towered high above their heads. It was brilliantly lighted by a multitude of little tapers; and everywhere sparkled and glittered with bright objects. There were rosy-cheeked dolls, hiding behind the green leaves; and there were real watches (with movable hands, at least, and an endless capacity of being wound up) dangling from innumerable twigs; there were French-polished tables, chairs, bedsteads, wardrobes, eight-day clocks, and various other articles of domestic furniture (wonderfully made, in tin, at Wolverhampton), perched among the boughs, as if in preparation for some fairy housekeeping; there were jolly, broad-faced men, much more agreeable in appearance than many real men – and no wonder, for their heads took off, and showed them to be full of sugar-plums; there were fiddles and drums; there were tambourines, books, work-boxes, paint-boxes, sweetmeat boxes, peep-show boxes, and all kinds of boxes; there were trinkets for the elder girls, far brighter than any grown-up gold and jewels; there were baskets and pin-cushions in all devices; there were guns, swords and banners; there were witches standing in enchanted rings of pasteboard, to tell fortunes; there were tetotums, humming-tops, needle-cases, pen-wipers, smelling-bottles, conversation-cards, bouquet-holders; real fruit, made artificially dazzling with gold leaf; imitation apples, pears, and walnuts, crammed with surprises; in short, as a pretty child, before me, delightfully whispered to another pretty child, her bosom friend, 'There was everything, and more.'

from *A Christmas Tree*
CHARLES DICKENS

The Christmas morning church service is traditionally the high point of country Christmas celebrations, and here American writer Washington Irving brings to life one such occasion in the Yorkshire of the mid-nineteenth century:

While we were talking, we heard the distant toll of the village bell, and I was told that the squire was a little particular in having his household at church on a Christmas morning; considering it a day of pouring out of thanks and rejoicing; for, as old Tusser observed,

At Christmas be merry, and thankful withal,
And feast they poor neighbours, the great with the small.

'If you are disposed to go to church,' said Frank Bracebridge, 'I can promise you a specimen of my cousin Simon's musical achievements. As the church is destitute of an organ, he has formed a band from the village amateurs, and established a musical club for their improvement; he has also sorted a choir, as he sorted my father's pack of hounds, according to the directions of Jervaise Markham, in his *Country Contentments*; for the bass he has sought out all the "deep, solemn mouths," and for the tenor the "loud-ringing mouths," among the country bumpkins, and for "sweet mouths," he has culled with curious taste among the prettiest lasses in the neighbourhood; though these last, he affirms, are the most difficult to keep in tune; your pretty female singer being exceedingly wayward and capricious, and very liable to accident' . . .

The orchestra was in a small gallery, and presented a most whimsical grouping of heads, piled one above the other, among which I had particularly noticed that of the village tailor, a pale fellow with a retreating forehead and chin, who played on the clarionet, and seemed to have blown his face to a point; and there was another, a short pursy man, stooping and labouring at a bass-viol, so as to show nothing but the top of a round bald head, like the egg of an ostrich. There were two or three pretty faces among the female singers, to which the keen air of a frosty morning had given a bright rosy tint; but the gentlemen choristers had evidently been chosen, like old Cremona fiddles, more for tone than looks; and as several had to sing from the same book, there were clusterings of odd physiognomies, not unlike those groups of cherubs we sometimes see on country tombstones.

The usual services of the choir were managed tolerably well, the vocal parts generally lagging a little behind the instrumental, and some loitering fiddler now and then making up for lost time by travelling over a passage with prodigious celerity, and clearing more bars than the keenest fox-hunter to be in at the death. But the great trial was an anthem that had been prepared and arranged by Master Simon, and on which he had founded great expectation. Unluckily there was a blunder at the very onset; the musicians became flurried; Master Simon was in a fever; everything went on lamely and irregularly until they came to a chorus beginning 'Now let us sing with one accord,' which seemed to be a signal for parting company; all became discord and confusion; each shifted for himself, and got to the end as well, or rather, as soon as he could, excepting one old chorister in a pair of horn spectacles, bestriding and pinching a long sonorous nose, who happened to stand a little apart, and, being wrapped up in his own melody, kept on a quavering course, wriggling his head, ogling his book, and winding up all by a nasal solo of at least three bars' duration.

from *Old Christmas*
WASHINGTON IRVING

In North Yorkshire, world famous vet James Herriot made an urgent Christmas morning visit and received some unusual country hospitality:

Inside the tiny living-room of the cottage I was ushered to the best chair by the fireside where two rough logs blazed and crackled.

'Bring cake out for Mr Herriot, mother,' the farmer cried as he rummaged in the pantry. He reappeared with a bottle of whisky at the same time as his wife bustled in carrying a cake thickly laid with icing and ornamented with coloured spangles, toboggans, reindeers.

Mr Kirby unscrewed the stopper. 'You know, mother, we're lucky to have such men as this to come out on a Christmas mornin' to help us.'

'Aye, we are that.' The old lady cut a thick slice of the cake and placed it on a plate by the side of an enormous wedge of Wensleydale cheese . . .

I took a bite of the cake and followed it with a moist slice of cheese. When I had first come to Yorkshire I had been aghast when offered this unheard-of combination, but time had brought wisdom and I had discovered that the mixture when chewed boldly together was exquisite; and, strangely, I had also found that there was nothing more suitable for washing it finally over the tonsils than a draught of raw whisky.

'You don't mind t'wireless, Mr Herriot?' Mrs Kirby asked. 'We always like to have it on Christmas morning to hear t'old hymns but I'll turn it off if you like.'

'No, please leave it, it sounds grand.' I turned to look at the old radio with its chipped wooden veneer, the orante scroll-work over the worn fabric; it must have been one of the earliest models and it gave off a tinny sound, but the singing of the church choir was none the less sweet . . . 'Hark the Herald Angels Sing' – flooding the little room, mingling with the splutter of the logs and the soft voices of the old people.

from *Let Sleeping Vets Lie*
JAMES HERRIOT

THE FEAST

The centrepiece of the Christmas feast is meat and traditionally the best the family can afford. In Northern Europe wild boar was originally the favoured sacrificial animal for the grand feasts, and was served on a dish of gold or silver in great pomp and ceremony. The custom lives on at Queen's College, Oxford, where a boar's head is served to a variation of the old carol:

Caput apri defero, Reddens laudens Domino.
The boar's head in hand bring I
With garlands gay and rosemary:
I pray you all sing merrily,
Qui estis in convivio . . .

Hone's Book of Days gives us the history:

'The custom sprung, according to university legend, from a valorous act on the part of a student of the college in question. While walking in Shotover Forest, studying his Aristotle, he was suddenly made aware of the presence of a wild-boar, by the animal rushing at him open-mouthed. With great prescence of mind, and the exclamation, "*Graecum est*", the collegian thrust the philosopher's ethics down the assailant's throat, and having choked the savage with the sage, went on his way rejoicing.'

Distant relatives in the form of roast pork, sausages, and ham still feature at Christmas. The English developed a liking for roast beef, swans and peacocks, while the Austrians and Germans preferred goose. This was gradually introduced into Britain and Ireland, after it is said that one Christmas Eve Queen Elizabeth I was dining on goose when news of the victory over the Armada reached her and she declared it to be eaten at Christmas. However it wasn't long before turkeys were introduced from the New World, and by the early 19th century had all but taken over the Christmas markets.

The Christmas Pudding began life as a frumenty, a Christmas fasting dish, made of wheat boiled in milk and seasoned with spices and sugar, but gradually over the years meat, eggs, spirits, and dried fruits were added to evolve into a plum porridge. Eventually the meat was left out and the mixture thickened to become the pudding we know today. A sprig of holly is added as a symbol of everlasting life, and the burning brandy a reminder of the rebirth of the sun.

Sussex folk-singer and writer Bob Copper tells the wonderful story of how he and his brother Ron nearly lost the family Christmas dinner:

At home Christmas was still celebrated as whole-heartedly as it always had been in spite of the fact that Grand-dad had died in 1924. There was a very special feel about Christmas morning and right from the moment you woke up and even before you got out of bed you would hear Dad downstairs singing carols as he raked the ashes from the kitchen range. By the time you got downstairs, he would be lighting the fire in the front room and this was a sure sign that it was a very important day.

The job of taking the Christmas dinner down to the bake-house at the back of the Black Horse had been passed down a generation to Ron and me, and at about half-past seven we would set off with our precious load. We still had a huge round of beef every year, although it was no longer a present from the farmer as it had been in Grand-dad's day, and for the convenience of carrying this and the large turkey, together with an enamel dinner-can with a tight-fitting lid in which to bring home the dripping, Dad had made a wooden carrier like a stretcher about six feet long with two handles at each end. The bird

and the joint, thickly daubed with dripping, would be covered with grease-proof paper, then with several layers of clean corn sacks to keep in the heat on the return journey and finally draped with a white linen table cloth.

As we walked down to the village and turned into the almost deserted High Street, the funereal appearance of our burden would prompt suitable quips from the one or two men we did see. 'Let's 'ave a look at the ol' man afore y' screws 'im down' – 'You've come too far, en't ye? You've passed the grave-yard' or 'It's a shame, I say, t'lose a loved one at a time like Christmas.'

After breakfast, we would help Dad decorate the front room. He obviously loved every minute of Christmas and went joyfully about the task of slinging paper-chains from the corners of the room to the electric light rose in the centre of the ceiling, sticking holly behind the pictures on the wall and entwining runners of ivy round the turned columns of the elaborate mahogany over-mantel. Coloured glass baubles, carefully saved from year to year, were hung amongst the greenery and a blue and silver blown-glass peacock with a long tail of silken plumage occupied the centre of the room clipped to a carpenter's pencil stuck into the side of the light-fitting.

As he climbed each chair in turn reaching up to fasten a paper bell to the ceiling with a drawing pin or tuck another spray of yew behind the curtain rail, he would sing an appropriate snatch of song:

> *The mistletoe hung in the castle hall,*
> *The holly branch hung on the old oak wall,*
> *The Baron's retainers were blithe and gay*
> *All keeping their Christmas holiday . . .*

His mood was infectious and we joined in with both the decorating and the singing with enthusiasm . . .

By twelve o'clock on Christmas morning the front room was bedecked and burgeoning like a green forest glade. The sideboard was laden with bottles of port wine and sherry, bowls of tangerines and nuts and boxes of dried figs, dates and crystallized fruits, while a fire crackled merrily in the hearth. Mother and two or three odd aunties were busy in the scullery cooking vegetables

and preparing sauces and all the attendant etceteras without which the main ingredient – gently browning in Mr Hilder's oven – would not be fully appreciated, and steam from the Christmas pudding, as it bubbled gently in a large iron saucepan at the back of the hob, filled every nook and corner of the cottage with spicy, ambrosial aroma.

The company, mostly relatives, was beginning to assemble with everyone in a jovial mood and on their best behaviour, showing off the ties, socks, handkerchiefs, and pairs of gloves they had received as presents that morning and as the glasses of wine were handed round, a vibrant sense of warmth and good fellowship prevailed. There was an air of excitement and the women-folk were becoming intensely concerned with laying the three tables, one in the front room, one in the kitchen and another in the scullery (for the children) which were necessary to get everyone seated. They scuttled in and out with plates, glasses, cutlery, and cruets, arranging and re-arranging fussily until the spread met their critical approval. The men, in an expansive mood, talked of Christmases gone by with the seats of their trousers to the fire and handling their unaccustomed cigars like cows with muskets, while we, the small fry, were left pretty much to our own devices.

One year our devices included surreptitiously filling our glasses with sherry instead of ginger wine and the holiday spirit suddenly slipped into top gear. Life put on a great big smile and Ron and I laughed and skylarked all the way down to the bakehouse to fetch the turkey and joint of beef. On the journey home with our succulent load swinging between us I had an inspiration. There had been a pretty sharp frost that morning and the pond was frozen over. One or two small children had been tentatively testing the strength of the ice but the chances of it bearing any substantial weight were slim. 'Ron,' I said, all valiant with sherry, 'we've never took the ol' bird across the pond before. Let's give 'er a try, shall us?' Ron mumbled dissenting noises behind me but as I was in the leading shafts he had no option but to follow me.

Gingerly easing one shiny, brown shoe in front of the other I edged forward on to the yielding ice. Ron kept up a rumble of protest at the back but I pushed on over the undulating surface. 'The more she bends the more she bears,' I cried. I was feeling buoyantly confident and we were already more than halfway across. 'Come on, we're goin' t' make 'istory t'day, ol' kiddy,' I said. 'Yeah,' was the sardonic reply, 'we'll make 'istory all right, if we drop the bloody lot in the pond.'

Just then there was a fusillade of sound like rifle fire and I dropped through the ice and stood knee-deep in freezing water. The stretcher tilted dangerously and the two dishes started to slide forward and were only saved from a watery grave by Ron slowly sinking down behind me till he stood in the mud on the same level as I, restoring the stretcher to an even keel. It was a fearful moment. We took stock and, ignoring the state of our clothes, were thankful enough that the dinner was still intact.

With the crisis over, we sploshed ashore and on to the bank where, with handfuls of grass, we wiped off the worst of the creamy, grey mud with which our best shoes and the trouser legs of our Sunday suits were plastered. 'I told y' it wouldn't bear,' said Ron as we squelched up the road leaving a sad, dripping trail behind us.

Back in the cottage the state of our clothes passed unnoticed in the excitement and bustle of dishing up what was generally considered to be the meal of the year. It was an unqualified success and, as we looked round at the happy faces munching away ecstatically at the loaded plates before them, we observed a diplomatic silence about how narrowly their dinner had avoided finishing up at the bottom of the duck-pond. Ron gave me a knowing wink and we tucked another guilty secret under our belts alongside the stolen gooseberries and Miss Macintosh's cat.

The evening was dedicated to singing with perhaps a perfunctory game of whist going on between the ladies in the corner. With Dad and Uncle John in the seats of honour on each side of the fireplace – the positions once occupied by Grand-dad and great Uncle Tom – we sang the carols and Christmas hymns with a zest and enthusiasm undiminished over the years. All the old rules were still strictly observed including 'every song a drink' but 'no spirits on the table till half past nine' by which time the carols and hymns had all been sung and we began to branch out into all the old favourites, usually starting with 'The Twelve Days of Christmas'. I sat by Uncle John modelling my singing on his while Ron was over with Dad, his mentor, providing the bass section or 'heavy brigade'.

The songs flowed like a river and as Christmas night developed into Boxing morning and we curled up on the sofa, in the narrow space not occupied by avuncular backsides, and drifted close to sleep, the old familiar and melodious sounds went on. By sheer weight of numbers, as well as an inborn affection, these old songs were being driven into the very marrow of our bones.

from Early to Rise – A Sussex Boyhood
BOB COPPER

WILTSHIRE CAROL

Trad. arr. J. Coppin ©

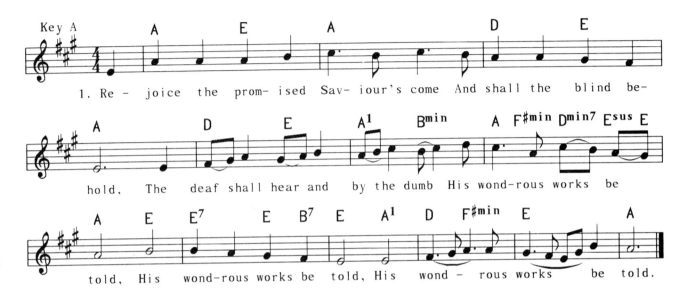

1. Re - joice the prom- ised Sav- iour's come And shall the blind be- hold, The deaf shall hear and by the dumb His wond-rous works be told, His wond-rous works be told, His wond - rous works be told.

2. Light from the sacred shore shall spread,
O'er all the world shall beam,
In pastures fair shall all be led,
And drink of comfort's stream.
And drink of comfort's stream,
And drink of comfort's stream.

3. The weary nations shall have rest,
The rage of war shall cease,
The earth with innocence be blest,
And plenty dwell with peace.
And plenty dwell with peace,
And plenty dwell with peace.

This unusual and little known carol has a universal message of peace. The tune and words were collected by the Rev. Geoffrey Hill from the village of Britford and published in Wiltshire Folk Songs and Carols 1898. *I am indebted to Jean Morrison and Celia Cologne who included it in their* Wiltshire Folk Songs, *and to Geoff Elwell for bringing it to my attention.*

Even the inmates of some workhouses were able to join in the Christmas feasting, but not without disapproval. This article is from the *Essex Standard* of 1 January 1841:

This year the poor of the Union Houses of Chelmsford, Halstead, Maldon and Rochford, received an extra allowance on Christmas Day. At Braintree, the inmates of the House had roast beef and plum pudding, a pint of strong beer for each adult, half a pint for each child; pipes, tobacco and snuff were also given. Pretty doings at Braintree truly!

At Romford to the disgrace of the Guardians, the paupers, 400 in number had 240 plum puddings, weighing in all 600 lbs.

What an uproar these proceedings will make at Somerset House. Paupers eating plum puddings on Christmas Day!

What will the world come to?

It was Christmas Day in the Workhouse
And the cold bare walls are bright
With garlands of green and holly
And the place is a pleasant sight
For with clean washed hands and faces
In a long and hungry line
The paupers sit at the tables
For this is the hour they dine.

And the Guardians and their ladies
Although the wind is east
Have come in their furs and wrappers
To watch their charges feast
To smile and be condescending
Put pudding on paupers's plates
To be hosts at the Workhouse banquet
They've paid for – with the rates . . .

GEORGE R. SIMS

Back from the morning church service, Washington Irving then enjoyed an old-fashioned Christmas dinner with his Yorkshire hosts:

THE CHRISTMAS DINNER

A sideboard was set out on which was a display of plate that might have vied (at least in variety) with Belshazzar's parade of the vessels of the temple; 'flagons, cans, cups, beakers, goblets, basins, and ewers'; the gorgeous utensils of good companionship, that had gradually accumulated through many generations of jovial housekeepers. Before these stood the two Yule candles beaming like two stars of the first magnitude; other lights were distributed in branches, and the whole array glittered like a firmament of silver.

We were ushered into this banqueting scene with the sound of minstrelsy, the old harper being seated on a stool beside the fireplace, and twanging his instrument with a vast deal more power then melody. Never did Christmas board display a more goodly and gracious assemblage of countenances: those who were not handsome were, at least, happy; and happiness is a rare improver of your hard favoured visage.

The parson said grace, which was not a short familiar one, such as is commonly addressed to the Deity, in these unceremonious days; but a long, courtly, well worded one of the ancient school. There was now a pause, as if something was expected; when suddenly the butler entered the hall with some degree of bustle: he was attended by a servant on each side with a large wax light, and bore a silver dish, on which was an enormous pig's head decorated with rosemary, with a lemon in its mouth, which was placed with great formality at the head of the table. The moment this pageant made its appearance, the harper struck up a flourish; at the conclusion of which the young Oxonian, on receiving a hint from the squire, gave, with an air of the most comic gravity, an old carol.

Though prepared to witness many of these little eccentricities, from being apprised of the peculiar hobby of mine host; yet, I confess, the parade with which so odd a

dish was introduced somewhat perplexed me, until I gathered from the conversation of the squire and the parson that it was meant to represent the bringing in of the boar's head: a dish formerly served up with much ceremony, and the sound of minstrelsy and song, at great tables on Christmas day. 'I like the old custom,' said the squire, 'not merely because it is stately and pleasing in itself, but because it was observed at the College of Oxford, at which I was educated. When I hear the old song chanted, it brings to mind the time when I was young and gamesome – and the noble old college hall – and my fellow students loitering about in their black gowns; many of whom, poor lads, are now in their graves!'

The table was literally loaded with good cheer, and presented an epitome of country abundance, in this season of overflowing larders. A distinguished post was allotted to 'ancient sirloin,' as mine host termed it; being, as he added, 'the standard of old English hospitality, and a joint of goodly presence, and full of expectation'. There were several dishes quaintly decorated, and which had evidently something traditionary in their embellishments; but about which, as I did not like to appear over-curious, I asked no questions.

I could not, however, but notice a pie, magnificently decorated with peacocks' feathers, in imitation of the tail of that bird, which overshadowed a considerable tract of the table. This the squire confessed, with some little hesitation, was a pheasant pie, though a peacock pie was certainly the most authentical; but there had been such a mortality among the peacocks this season, that he could not prevail upon himself to have one killed.

When the cloth was removed, the butler brought in a huge silver vessel of rare and curious workmanship, which he placed before the squire. Its appearance was hailed with acclamation; being the Wassail Bowl, so renowned in Christmas festivity. The contents had been prepared by the squire himself; for it was a beverage in the skilful mixture of which he particularly prided himself; alleging that it was too abstruse and complex for the comprehension of an ordinary servant. It was a potation, indeed, that might well make the heart of a toper leap within him; being composed of the richest and raciest wines, highly spiced and sweetened, with roasted apples bobbing about the surface.

The old gentleman's whole countenance beamed with a serene look of indwelling delight, as he stirred this mighty bowl. Having raised it to his lips, with a hearty wish of a merry Christmas to all present, he sent it brimming round the board, for every one to follow his example, according to the primitive style; pronouncing it 'the ancient fountain of good feeling, where all hearts met together'.

from *Old Christmas*
WASHINGTON IRVING

CHRISTMAS

Christmas has come, let's eat and drink –
This is no time to sit and think;
Farewell to study, books and pen,
And welcome to all kinds of men.
Let all men now get rid of care,
And what one has let others share;
Then 'tis the same, no matter which
Of us is poor, or which is rich.
Let each man have enough this day,
Since those that can are glad to pay;
There's nothing now too rich or good
For poor men, not the King's own food.
Now like a singing bird my feet
Touch earth, and I must drink and eat.
Welcome to all men: I'll not care
What any of my fellows wear;
We'll not let cloth divide our souls,
They'll swim stark naked in the bowls.
Welcome, poor beggar: I'll not see
That hand of yours dislodge a flea,–
While you sit at my side and beg,
Or right foot scratching your left leg.
Farewell restraint: we will not now
Measure the ale our brains allow,
But drink as much as we can hold.
We'll count no change when we spend gold;
This is no time to save, but spend,
To give for nothing, not to lend.
Let foes make friends: let them forget
The mischief-making dead that fret
The living with complaint like this –
'He wronged us once, hate him and his.'
Christmas has come; let every man
Eat, drink, be merry all he can.
Ale's my best mark, but if port wine
Or whisky's yours – let it be mine;
No matter what lies in the bowls,
We'll make it rich with our own souls.
Farewell to study, books and pen,
And welcome to all kinds of men.

W. H. DAVIES

Dylan Thomas has some wonderful childhood memories of Christmas in Wales:

One Christmas was so much like another, in those years, around the sea-town corner now, and out of all sound except the distant speaking of the voices I sometimes hear a moment before sleep, that I can never remember whether it snowed for six days and six nights when I was twelve or whether it snowed for twelve days and twelve nights when I was six; or whether the ice broke and the skating grocer vanished like a snowman through a white trap-door on that same Christmas Day that the mince-pies finished Uncle Arnold and we tobogganed down the seaward hill, all the afternoon, on the best tea-tray, and Mrs Griffiths complained, and we threw a snowball at her niece, and my hands burned so, with the heat and the cold, when I held them in front of the fire, that I cried for twenty minutes and then had some jelly.

All the Christmases roll down the hill towards the Welsh-speaking sea, like a snowball growing whiter and bigger and rounder, like a cold and headlong moon bundling down the sky that was our street; and they stop at the rim of the ice-edged, fish-freezing waves, and I plunge my hands in the snow and bring out whatever I can find; holly or robins or pudding, squabbles and carols and oranges and tin whistles, and the fire in the front room, and bang go the crackers, and holy, holy, holy, ring the bells, and the glass bells shaking on the tree, and Mother Goose, and Struwelpeter – oh! the baby-burning flames and the clacking scissorman! – Billy Bunter and Black Beauty, Little Women and boys who have three helpings, Alice and Mrs Potter's badgers, penknives, teddy-bears – named after a Mr Theodore Bear, their inventor, or father, who died recently in the United States – mouth-organs, tin-soldiers, and blancmange, and Auntie Bessie playing 'Pop Goes the Weasel' and 'Nuts in May' and 'Oranges and Lemons' on the untuned piano in the parlour all through the thimble-hiding musical-chairing blind-man's-buffing party at the end of the never-to-be-forgotten day at the end of the unremembered year.

from *Miscellany*
DYLAN THOMAS

It's easy to forget that not only does farming have to carry on over Christmas, but sea-fishing too. Here Charles Kingsley paints a vivid picture of Christmas Day on the North Devon coast with the winter storms about to break:

'HOW AMYAS KEPT HIS CHRISTMAS DAY'

It was the blessed Christmas afternoon. The light was fading down; the even-song was done; and the good folks of Bideford were trooping home in merry groups, the father with his children, the lover with his sweetheart, to cakes and ales, and flapdragons and mummer's plays, and all the happy sports of Christmas night. One lady only, wrapped close in her black muffler, and followed by her maid, walked swiftly, yet sadly, toward the long causeway and bridge which led to Northam town. Sir Richard Grenville and his wife caught her up and stopped her courteously.

'You will come home with us, Mrs Leigh,' said Lady Grenville, 'and spend a pleasant Christmas night?'

Mrs Leigh smiled sweetly, and laying one hand on Mrs Grenville's arm, pointed with the other to the westward, and said, –

'I cannot well spend a merry Christmas night while that sound is in my ears.'

But what was the sound that troubled Mrs Leigh? None of them, with their merry hearts, and ears dulled with the din and bustle of the town, had heard it till that moment; and yet now – listen! It was dead calm. There was not a breath to stir a blade of grass. And yet the air was full of sound – a low, deep roar which hovered over down and wood, salt marsh and river, like a roll of a thousand wheels, the tramp of endless armies, or – what it was – the thunder of a mighty surge upon the boulders of the pebble ridge.

'The ridge is noisy to-night,' said Sir Richard. 'There has been wind somewhere.'

'There is wind now, where my boy is, God help him!' said Mrs Leigh; and all knew that she spoke truly. The spirit of the Atlantic storm had sent forward the token of his coming, in the smooth ground-swell which was heard

SAILOR'S CAROL

Words: Charles Causley/Music J. Coppin ©

1. Lord, the snow full sky In this pale Dec-emb-er Fing-ers my clear eye Lest see-ing, I rem-emb-er. Not the nak-ed ba-by Wee-ping in the stab-le, Nor the sing-ing boys All round my tab-le, Not the dizz-y star Burst-ing on the pane Nor the leop-ard sun Paw-ing the rain. On-ly the deep gard-en Where green lil-ies grow, The sail-ors roll-ing in the sea's blue snow.

Charles Causley was born in Cornwall, and served in the Royal Navy. This poem like much of his work is a wonderful mix of religious and seafaring images.

inland, two miles away. Tomorrow the pebbles, which were now rattling down with each retreating wave, might be leaping up to the ridge top, and hurled like round-shot far ashore upon the marsh by the force of the advancing wave, fleeing before the wrath of the western hurricane.

'God help my boy!' said Mrs Leigh again.

'God is as near him by sea as by land,' said good Sir Richard.

'True, but I am a lone mother, and one that has no heart just now but to go home and pray.'

And so Mrs Leigh went onward up the lane, and spent all that night in listening between her prayers to the thunder of the surge, till it was drowned, long ere the sun rose, in the thunder of the storm.

His mother's presage had been true enough. Christmas Eve had been the last of the still, dark, steaming nights of early winter; and the western gale has been roaring for the last twelve hours upon the Irish coast.

CHRISTMAS DAY GAMES AND CUSTOMS

As well as the usual indoor Christmas Day games of charades, board games and cards, there are a few unusual traditions. Swimming in the sea on Christmas Day still occurs at many places such as Hunstanton and the South Coast to raise money for charity.

At Penryn in Cornwall around 1884 there was a custom of Dancing round the Candles. Children used to sing and dance round lit candles, probably as a vestige of ancient fire rites associated with the winter solstice.

A football match used to be played in the streets of Kirkham in Lancashire in the early 1800s, and at Hornchurch in Essex, there was a traditional wrestling match and a boar's head was provided for the victor by the lessee of the tithes, New College, Oxford:

From Hone's Everyday Book

'On Christmas Day the following custom has been observed at Hornchurch, in Essex, from time immemorial. The lessee of the tithes, which belong to New College, Oxford, supplies a boar's head, dressed and garnished with bayleaves and such. In the afternoon, it is carried in procession into Mill Field, adjoining the church-yard, where it is wrestled for; and it is afterwards feasted upon at one of the public houses by the rustic conqueror and his friends, with all merriment peculiar to the season.'

In the fens of East Anglia, Edward Storey delights in the memory of an old-fashioned family Christmas Day, with games and stories of country characters:

'AS IT WAS'

After a quiet Christmas Eve I still have what is, I suppose, an old-fashioned Christmas, spending Christmas Day at the home of my parents with other members of the family. Sometimes there can be fourteen of us gathered round the table and each year the same games are played, the same stories told, the same memories brought out like the carols, decorations and nut-crackers to give the season its customary pattern. And always other Christmasses come back into our thoughts and conversations. When I watch my six-year-old nephew, David, I see quite clearly those Christmas Days I had when I was a child his age. The mystery of the old man with a red cloak and a white beard who somehow squeezed down our chimney with a sack of toys ceased to be a mystery in the morning when the bottom of the bed was loaded with presents. The thrill of waking early and rushing into my parents' bedroom with some of the toys, the excitement of going downstairs into a room that had been transformed during the night with a Christmas tree and coloured lights, the very taste of the home-made pork pie we had for breakfast, all come back to me as I see myself in this other child . . .

By the time breakfast was over the day was really alive. The radio would be loud with 'Christians Awake' or 'O Come all ye faithful' and final preparations for our

Christmas Dinner would put the small kitchen out of bounds as far as the children were concerned. Toy cannons shot down a troop of cavalrymen, a new fire-engine crashed into the piano, and happy shouts came from every part of the house. Into this confusion of noise, colour, crackers, balloons and humming-tops came my grand-parents to spend their Christmas quietly with us.

No one bothered how much coal or wood was put on the fire. The room just grew hotter and hotter. One year the paper decorations caught fire and all the balloons burst. There was a great fanning of arms and towels and stamping of feet. The room filled with a grey cloud of smoke that spread into a black snowstorm and I rushed out into the yard shouting 'Fire! Fire!'. There was no one to hear me. The neighbours were involved in their own fires. The forlorn white world outside looked cold and desolate. Only the birds had life as they pecked away at a few scraps that had been thrown out for them. They did not even look up as I waved my arms in an abortive attempt to raise the alarm. The sky was as expressionless as a frozen pond. The old wash-house at the bottom of the garden looked far away and forsaken. The water-tap was frozen and a long icicle hung there gnarled and white as candle-wax.

When my mother called me back into the house the panic was over. The smoke was disappearing through the open window and I could see quite clearly now the unperturbed outlines of the china dogs on the mantel-piece and the untroubled face of the wall clock. From the ceiling hung the wire skeletons of Chinese lanterns and the charred pieces of tape on which the balloons had blossomed.

'Would you like a game of draughts?' asked my grand-mother, as if nothing had happened, 'or Snakes and Ladders?'

This question made the fire only the beginning of the afternoon's fun or drama. The shake of the dice or the appearance of the cards or draught-board fanned flames that were just as dangerous, for my grandmother never liked to lose. If she saw that this was likely to happen she would accuse us all of cheating and throw the board up into the air so that no one could win.

Sometimes my grandparents would stay all day and sometimes they would leave later in the afternoon to have tea with one of my aunts. When they stayed all day some of my aunts, uncles and cousins would come to spend their evenings with us as well. Then the fun was four-fold and the events would be quite unpredictable. The table – a big round table that stood permanently in the centre of the room – would be cleared for cards, dominoes, or 'tippet' and the door to the stairs would be closed to take the dartboard. There would be singing and laughter and stories of local characters who haunted our Christmasses then like ghosts of long ago. If half the stories were true then no town has ever had more clowns, lunatics, drunks or eccentrics than ours.

I heard of strange old characters in the fens who were laws unto themselves – men who never washed from one year's end to another, who worked stripped to the waist even in winter and who wrestled with bulls for shilling bets. One uncle told a murder story while another uncle sang 'Ten Green Bottles'. I heard about the days when the King's Dyke Silver Prize Band went out carol-playing in snow so deep they lost their euphonium-player and how Flowery George tripped over his lantern and rolled into a ditch that extinguished them both. The same characters were talked about each year, characters whose idiosyncrasies earned them a place in the folk-lore of the town and won for them an affection that has been handed down from one generation to the next; characters who could turn a simple phrase into something quite extraordinary and memorable, such as 'I remember the first time I went up a ladder was down a well', or 'Without a word of a lie I know that's true 'cus I stood at my clock as the door struck twelve'.

The family laughed as they laughed each year and one story prompted another so that in the end everyone had recalled some favourite character. There was Billy Blunt and Rowdy Dick the drover, Porky Frost and Charlie Smack.

'The night I shall never forget,' I heard someone say, 'was that winter when we piled snow right up above Billy Cuckoo's front door and windows and then dropped a bottle down the chimney with a message in it which said

THE END IS NEAR. They reckon he was still praying when they dug 'im out three days later.'

'What about the night when old Rowdy Dick drove his bullocks into the police station to report them for being drunk and disorderly . . . '

'What about that time when Uncle 'Lijah came to stay and was still sober after eighteen pints . . . '

. . . My nephew and his sister, Karen, become bored with their new toys and say, 'I know, let's make a play. You be Red Riding Hood and I'll be the wolf.' And so the years and memories are lost in an hour of dramatizing the fairy stories that amuse them more than their toys or the television show. They mimic and make up lines as they go. They make costumes out of an assortment of scarves and build palaces out of old cardboard boxes. We act some of the plays three times over, each playing the different characters in turn. Into this confusion of noise, colour, crackers and balloons, *their* grand-parents came to spend a Christmas quietly with them.

from *A Solitary Landscape*
EDWARD STOREY

However down in Devon, June Smith (alias 'Martha') reminds us of the consequences of inviting relatives to stay:

Don't talk to me about relatives! I shall never forget last Christmas, never as long as I live. I asked Granny to stay. He can't stand the sight of my mother, but I wasn't going to take no notice of he so I wrote and asked Granny if her'd like to come for Christmas and Granny said her would. Well, he went up the village on Christmas Eve and met Granny off the bus with the pony and trap, and I put her to bed with a nice hot cup of cocoa. Then I said to Father, 'I think that I'll go to bed myself,' because Christmas, you know, is a busy old time.

I got half-way up the stairs and I realised I hadn't iced me cake. I'd made him like you should. Had him in a tin for about six weeks, I had, but I hadn't had time to ice him. So I come down and I said to Father, 'I can't have Granny sitting up to Christmas tea and no icing on the cake.' So, although I was tired, I got a basin, made a bit of icing and put it on top of the old cake. And then I said to Father – 'Oh what a pity! I haven't got nothing to put on him.' Well, he's got a push bike, so he said, 'Hang on a bit, Mother,' and he went out in the shed and he come in with a little old baccy tin with a few ball-bearings in him. So I washed them off and polished them up and put them around the edge of the cake, and, although I say so myself, the old cake didn't look bad. Then he had a brain-wave. He went behind the picture and broke off a bit of holly and us stuck it in the middle, and, although I say so meself, the cake looked handsome.

I went to bed happy that night. The turkey was in the dairy, all stuffed, Granny was tucked up in bed asleep, and the cake was all iced. Oh, I went to bed and slept well, I did. Well, us got up in the morning, did our work, went to church and had our dinner, and listened to the Queen. Father went out and milked the cows, and then it was tea-time.

I know that you should start with a bit of bread and butter, but granny asked for a bit of cake. I said to Father, 'Give her a nice big bit, there's plenty there,' so he did. He cut her a nice big bit of cake and her sat down and eat it and enjoyed it. Then darn me, if she didn't ask for another bit! I said to Father, 'Get on and give her another bit, plenty there,' so he did. He cut her another nice big bit of cake but us forgot to tell her about the balls. But it didn't seem to make no difference, because her eats without her teeth in, and her wobbled it about a bit and got it down alright. Well, then us went into the front room – we all do it every year don't we? Go into the front room and sit beside the fire and have a little glass of what you fancy, whether 'tis sherry or whether 'tis whisky or whether 'tis a little drop of home-made wine or a glass of cider. Then you have a fig, then you'll have a date, then you'll have a nut or two, then perhaps you have another drop of sherry, then you'll have an orange and then there's that old box of Turkish delight – 'tis eating all the time isn't it? Well, that was when disaster struck. Granny got up, went to poke the fire, passed wind and shot the cat!

from A Devon Country Christmas

LEGENDS AND SUPERSTITIONS

Legend has it that Samson's Stone near Kenfig in S. Wales was thrown by St Samson from Mawgan Mountain, and before cockcrow every Christmas morning, it is believed to uproot itself and wander down to the River Sker for a drink.

Following the calendar change of 1752, the many Legends of the Flowering of the Holy Thorn are now associated with 5 January – Old Christmas Eve.

SUPERSTITIONS

A child born on Christmas Eve or Christmas Day was likely to be good and beautiful, while a death in the parish during Christmas was thought to be a portent of many deaths during the coming year. In Worcestershire it was thought very unlucky to

sit down thirteen to the table at Christmas, unless one person was pregnant.

It was thought to be very unlucky to give your neighbour a light, or take fire out of the house at Christmas and New Year. Working on the farm was particularly unlucky as graphically illustrated in the traditional Herefordshire carol 'On Christmas Day' (see overleaf).

On Christmas Day

Trad. arr. J. Coppin/P. Burgess ©

2. 'O man, O man, what makes you plough
So hard upon the Lord's birthday?'
The farmer answered him with great speed;
'For the plough this day we have great need'.

3. His arms did quaver to and fro;
His arms did quaver, he could not plough.
The ground did open and lose him in,
Before he could repent of sin.

4. His wife and children are out of place,
His beasts and cattle they die away;
His beasts and cattle they die away,
For the breaking of our Lord's birthday.

A traditional carol from Herefordshire on the perils of ploughing on Christmas Day. It was collected from the singing of Esther Smith at Dilwyn nr. Weobley by Ella Mary Leather & R. Vaughan Williams, and published in their Twelve Traditional Carols from Herefordshire *in 1920.*

WEATHERLORE

In Worcestershire sunshine on Christmas Day foretells many fires in the coming year. In Devon – 'Hours of sun on Christmas Day, so many frosts in the month of May' – and a widespread saying from Shropshire, and many other counties ran:

If the sun shines through the apple trees upon a Christmas Day,
when Autumn comes they will a load of fruit display.

Great importance is attached to the weather on Christmas Day as it is said to forecast the year's weather – 'a green Christmas, a white Easter' – and 'a green Christmas makes a fat churchyard' were well known sayings at one time throughout England and Scotland as fine weather was a portent of a very hard winter.

Other sayings were 'If the ice bear a man before Christmas, it will not bear a mouse after'; in Lincolnshire they believed 'a light Christmas, a light harvest', but in Somerset 'a light Christmas a heavy sheaf'. There would be a good harvest if snow covered the apple trees.

The day of the week on which Christmas Day fell was important in weather-forecasting. In Wales 'if Christmas on a Sunday be, a windy winter we shall see', while in England a Saturday Christmas was supposed to bring a foggy winter and a cold summer, and a Thursday a windy winter and a warm, dry summer.

Another belief was that the weather on each of the twelve days corresponded with the following months of the year.

A CHRISTMAS REVEL

I have seen a court, and a dozen courts,
And no court have I seen as gracious
As the court I love for its chieftain's sake,
Not weak is my praise, like Celliwig:
Heaven's bounty on earth in Bachelldref,
Where there is a revel each Christmas,
A crowd of kinsmen, a lake of liquor,
Bright the honour of Meurig's homeland,
Many a minstrel and merry fiddler,
And much the mirth on a polished floor,
And a sound of strings, a deluge of drinks,
And the constant cadence of singing,
And a red-hued lance of Cadwaladr's line,
A blood-gushing blade, promise of meat,
And minstrels' swaying, and children chirping,
And the bustle of boys bringing food,
The cup-bearer weary, kitchen sore-tried,
And three kinds of wine for the thirsty.
Three customs there are, a merry country,
At Dafydd's high court, blameless boldness;
Whoever you are, whatever you sing,
And whatever the thing you're known for,
Come whenever you wish, take what you see,
And once come, stay as long as you like.

DAFYDD BACH AP MADOG WLADAIDD
FL. 1340–1390

BOXING DAY AND AFTER

'The Wren, the Wren, the King of all Birds
St Stephen's Day was caught in the furze.'

THE CAMPDEN CAROL

Trad. arr: J. Coppin/P. Burgess ©

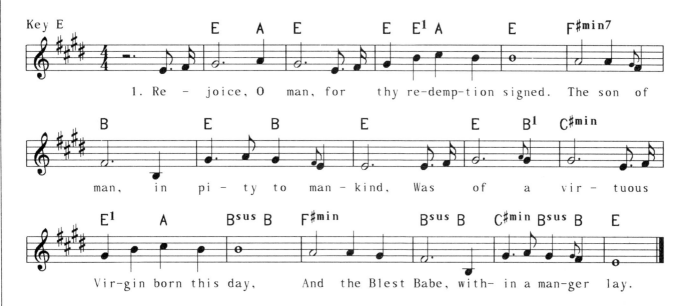

1. Re - joice, O man, for thy re-demp-tion signed. The son of man, in pi - ty to man - kind, Was of a vir - tuous Vir-gin born this day, And the Blest Babe, with- in a man-ger lay.

2. 'Twas strange that they, no room could find within
To entertain their Saviour and their King;
Who came from Heaven, for to redeem us all
From sin and death, entailed by Adam's fall.

3. Good St Stephen did a martyr die;
A crown of glory, he did gain thereby.
By suff'ring death, which proved to him, no loss,
Because he meekly bore his Master's cross.

4. And now in Heaven, in Heaven he doth remain
To wear a crown of glory, for his pain.
And every man shall have the same reward,
Who lays his life down, for his Lord.

From Chipping Campden in Gloucestershire, this carol was handed down by word of mouth, probably from mediaeval times. I came across the words and a fragment of the tune in Gloucester Library, and together with Paul Burgess completed the melody. The carol is actually two in one: the first two verses were sung on Christmas Eve, and the last two for St Stephen late on Christmas Day in the evening. Both carols were sung to the same tune.

Boxing Day/St Stephen's Day

The term Boxing Day has two possible origins. At one time it was the day that alms boxes, placed in churches over Christmas, were opened and their contents distributed, and also when servants and apprentices broke open small boxes containing tips from their masters and their customers. Today we still have the tradition of tipping, or giving 'Christmas boxes' to postmen, dustmen, and paper boys and girls. The day commemorates two St Stephens; one was the first Christian martyr, and the other, a ninth-century missionary in Sweden, and the patron saint of horses. The day has always been devoted to horses, hunting and shooting.

Until the eighteenth century horses and cattle were bled for medical reasons and it was thought to be beneficial to all draught animals.

'If you bleed your nag on St Stephen's Day,
He'll work your wark for ever and A'
is an old Wiltshire saying, while
'Yet Christmas be passed, then let horse be let blood,
For many a purpose it dooth them much good'
comes from Derbyshire.

Some horses were ridden into church to be blessed by the priest, or fed consecrated corn and the Horse's Prayer was often recited by children on St Stephen's Day:

Up the hill, beat me not,
Down the hill, hurry me not,
On the plain, spare me not,
In my stall, forget me not.

Racing

From the 1880s to 1914, pony-drawn coster-mongers' barrows were raced from the Swan pub in Newmarket Rd, Cambridge to Bottisham and back, a distance for five miles for a £1 prize. A small entrance fee was charged to raise money for Addenbrooke's Hospital.

Rural Sports and Hunting

The Boxing Day Meets of foxhunters were more social gatherings than for serious hunting. At Christmas time there is a tradition known all over Europe that the souls of the dead can be heard crossing the sky in the form of a ghostly pack of hounds. Wales, Exmoor and Dartmoor are among the places of Britain with the most sightings.

Bert Butler certainly never forgot the time he volunteered as a beater for a Boxing Day shoot in the Cotswolds:

'A DAY OUT WITH THE TOFFS'

Rarely now do we hear a man being called a 'Toff,' but in my boyhood, this term of affection and respect, was often on our lips. And we knew the would-be toffs, the masqueraders who were wide of the mark, but did not know it. It was, and probably still is, impossible to deceive a countryman. He knows what's what, and will in a trice, mentally demote the imposter. Even the boys had this social know-how, and the Sudeley Choirboys, more so than most of our school fellows.

It was after Christmas Day mattins in St Mary's Church, 1918, that the four top boys of Sudeley Choir, were asked if they would be willing to join the beaters, for a Boxing Day shooting party, on the extensive Sudeley estate. None of us realised what lay ahead for us, but it sounded exciting, all four of us agreed to be at the castle at nine-o'clock the next morning. My father said that the venture would half kill me, for I would have to tramp over miles of rough country, and there would be no chance to turn back.

Not one whit discouraged by Dad's remarks, I spent Christmas afternoon seeking a good stick, in Corndean Lane. I had enough sense to choose one of ash, that would last the whole day. Two other Winchcombe lads joined the beaters, and one of them brought an elderberry stick of that years growth. It would not last ten minutes! The experienced beaters poured scorn on the boy and the stick, all the invective they could think of, and us choirboys were not spared their kind of humour.

They said that we ought to wear our cassocks and surplices, and that they would be torn to shreds, before we emerged from the first wood! Also, they said that mostly likely, we would be mistaken for rabbits, and be shot! It was a relief when the toffs came from the castle, and the whole caboodle moved off across the fields, with all nonsense silenced. We soon learnt that the master of ceremonies was not the squire, but the head keeper. He

had his plan for the shoot, well thought out, and the toffs, like us, obeyed his orders.

My mother had given me a packet of her home-made ginger biscuits, substantial and 'moreish'. These, she said, were to munch as I walked along with the gang, and thus leave my haversack grub untouched for mid-day. My first mistake was to be too eager to carry the slain birds. In this folly, I was encouraged by the older, experienced beaters, and was soon overburdened with pheasants – which to my horror, had to be carried by their necks.

When I picked up my first capture by its legs, a beater of long experience, told me that had the keeper seen this, I would have felt his extra stout stick across my backside!

Now that I knew that dead pheasants must be carried by the neck, I regretted more than ever, my novice eagerness to grab the fallen birds. One would not expect a boy to be fussy as to the cleanliness of his hands, but those blood-soaked necks revolted me, and of course I had no chance to rub my blooded hands in grass, dry leaves, or on the trunk of a tree. Unofficial, self-appointed keepers, kept yelling 'Keep in line'. Easier said than done. Because of the Great War years, the woods on Sudeley estate had lacked the usual care and control, and keeping in line was a nightmare, to me anyway.

'Haggled to death' with dead pheasants, my haversack slip-sliding all over the place on my back, and trying all the time to come round to my chest, I barged through brambles, went sprawling over concealed fallen tree trunks, was whipped in the face by vicious branches, and all the while hanging on to the birds. This was no job for a choirboy! Hungry as a hunter, and no chance to get at the ginger biscuits. Dad knew what he was talking about, after all!

Emerging from that woodland horror, I was able to hand my birds to a man with a pony trap. It was his job to collect the game, so I let him have mine, and welcome! Youngsters have to learn, and mostly by the hard way. During the next drive, when the artful ones called out 'here you are, young un.' I yelled back, 'no fear, that's your bird.'

Now I could really use my ash beating stick, and enjoy walloping the tree trunks and feel that I was 'getting some of my own back.' Still the cry went up, 'Keep in line, you silly b . . . keep in line.' Exasperated by one with a very big mouth, I yelled back, 'keep in line yourself, you be yards in front, most of the time.' A choirboy giving tongue!

The toffs had arranged for their luncheon baskets to be brought to Waterhatch Farm, and no doubt that their fare was better than ours.

We were all tired and hungry, so all our uncouth sandwiches were eaten with relish. A big jug of scalding-hot tea would have been more than welcome, but none appeared. I could have slept like the log on which I sat to wolf my grub, and would willingly have 'called it a day' but there was no hope turning back.

Foolishly I said that there could be little more ground to cover after lunch. Wishful thinking that did me no good. The veteran beaters told me that I had seen nothing so far. The real shooting and the worst beating, always came in the afternoon. We had Willis's Coppice, Spoonley Wood and The Parks still to do! They said that the shoot would most likely end at Belas Knap!

Boxing Day is one of the shortest in the year, but this one was about the longest I ever knew. We went nowhere near Belas Knap. Had we done so, I might have cut loose, and have legged it down Corndean Lane to my home.

The whole caboodle arrived back at the castle at dusk, and the beaters were thanked and paid. The boys were given three shillings and a rabbit. Three shillings, and all at one go! We were mightily pleased, and our weariness vanished. My satisfaction and reward for that Boxing Day, was far beyond that of the toffs, the keeper, or the beaters, for I have always kept the memory of it evergreen.

from *A Cotswold Rag-Bag*
BERT BUTLER

WINTER: EAST ANGLIA

In a frosty sunset
So fiery red with cold
The footballers' onset
Rings out glad and bold;
Then boys from daily tether
With famous dogs at heel
In starlight meet together
And to farther hedges steal;
Where the rats are pattering
In and out the stacks,
Owls with hatred chattering
w oop at the terriers' backs.
And, frost forgot, the chase grows hot
Till a rat's foolish prize,
But the cornered weasel stands his ground,
Shrieks at the dogs and boys set round,
Shrieks as he knows they stand all round,
And hard as winter dies.

EDMUND BLUNDEN

SHOOTING OF SMALL BIRDS, RABBITING AND SQUIRREL HUNTING

It was commonly believed in the North of England, that the game laws were not in force on the 26 December.

Squirrels were hunted in Suffolk and many other counties for food and to control numbers. In Hampshire this was known as 'squoyling', a 'squoyle' or 'snog' being the name of the short weighted stick thrown at the squirrels to knock them out of the trees.

HUNTING THE WREN

St Stephen's Day was known as 'Wrenning day,' and the hunting the wrens was common practice at one time throughout Cornwall, Wales, Cleveland, Cumbria and Ireland. A wren was captured and killed, and carried from house to house to collect money – often to fund a party. There are various theories as to why this sacrificial ritual occurred throughout Europe. One is that it was the singing of the wren that gave St Stephen away, and another that this was the only day you could kill the king of all the birds. The wren was regarded as king because of a legend telling of how it won the contest to see which bird could fly the highest. Just when the eagle was about to win, the wren, who had been perched on the eagle's back, spread its wings to fly higher than any other bird.

On the Isle of Man, the wren was freely hunted in the 1800s. It was believed that a siren of the sea, who had lured sailors to their death by her singing, could only escape her avengers by turning into a wren. Men carried one or more dead wrens in a decorated cage around the houses and asked for money. A wren's feather was given to anyone who gave money, and possession of this feather was believed to avert the dangers of shipwreck.

Farm boys in Essex would wrap the wrens in silk ribbons, and go round the houses singing:

The Wren, the Wren, the King of all Birds
St Stephen's Day was caught in the furze
Although he be little his honour is great
Therefore good people, give us a treat . . .

In Ireland, the wren was carried on a holly bush, and even today Wren Boys go from house to house carrying a decorated bush, singing the Wren Song and collecting money. The wren is called 'the Devil's bird' because during the rebel-lion in the North, a group of English soldiers were being surrounded while they lay asleep, but were awoken by wrens pecking on their drums and managed to escape.

Alice Taylor has a particularly vivid recollection of the custom in her part of west Ireland:

We awoke that morning to a white, silent world. The light in the bedroom had a strange yellow-white hue from the reflected brightness of the snow. Through the bedside window we could see the trees in the grove outside: overnight they had been transformed from a dark green military formation into a still, white, pristine presence. Normally these trees rustled and whispered among themselves and birds were always on the move amongst them, but now there was no movement. Beautiful but lifeless, they were silent white statues and their snow-laden branches resembled the outstretched arms of graceful ballerinas. Not a bird was to be seen or heard . . .

The front window looked out over white fields which stretched down to the river valley; from there the land rose again and the farms on the hill across the river faced us and the farmhouses seemed to have shrunk in size beneath the snow; this white land rolled away into distant hills and on the far horizon we could see the white outline of the Kerry mountains. The hedges on the hill across the river were huddled under the snow and the sheep down in the river valley were the only sign of life in the whole scene. Contrasted with the brilliance of the snow, their colour had changed to yellow.

Then into our silent world came the sound of music coming down the boreen. The Wren Boys! We had forgotten about them with the excitement of the snow. We peered out the window, straining for a sight of them, but as yet the only sign of them was the music. It rolled over the silent farmyard and James, our old horse, gave a nervous neigh in the stable at this sudden intrusion of sound into his quiet corner. In the surrounding silence of the snow, the sound of the melodeon vibrated richly, filling the air with a charge of activity. No footsteps could be heard in the padded underfoot conditions, so we had only the music by which to judge their advance. As it grew louder we held our breath and then they burst into the quiet yard where their outrageous costumes contrasted vividly with the white background. There were about eight of them, dressed in all kinds of odd-looking garments: tall, long-legged men disguised in women's skirts and coats turned inside out, and girls in their fathers' pants hitched up with safety pins and bits of twine. They all had their faces blackened or covered in cloths with cut-outs for the mouth and eyes, and on their heads was an amazing range of hats and caps. The leader carried the melodeon and they trouped behind him as they approached the front door, laughing and jostling each other. They started to chant:

> The wran, the wran, the king of all birds,
> St Stephen's Day was caught in the furze;
> Up with the kettle and down with the pan
> And give us some money to bury the wran.

We ran from the bedroom to the top of the stairs from where we could watch them in action. They filed into the kitchen, making sure that their faces were well covered to preserve their disguise. The man with the melodeon sat on a chair beside the stairs and the rest of them lined up to dance a set to his music. They bounced off the stone floor and at first the snow flew in all directions from their boots and wellingtons. As they whirled around we tried to guess who they were. We had no problem in identifying one man who towered over the rest and danced with his back poker-straight and his knees almost hitting his jaw; Dan commented loudly that he was like a gate-pillar in motion. Though we realised that they must all be neighbours well known to us, still it was difficult to put names on them. As the music continued I watched the fingers flying up and down the keys of the melodeon and realised that I had watched those fingers many times and that they belonged to our friend Martin, but there was no way I was going to let him know that I had recognised

him. When the set was over, one of them sang a song in a disguised voice, which sent his companions into convulsions of laughter. As they filed out, the last to go held out a cap for any contribution that might be forthcoming. My mother gave each group of wren boys the same donation, but my father believed that the better the performance the bigger the reward.

After a hurried breakfast we got ourselves dressed up to go hunting the wren. It was the first year that I was considered old enough to survive a day on the wren trail and I was thrilled to bits to be taking part rather than just observing. Every year I had watched the wren boys come to our house and had wanted to join in the dressing up and the jaunt around the countryside. I got into my brother's pants and an old discarded coat of my father's and covered my face in an old tea towel with cut-out holes to avoid suffocation and donned my father's cap turned back to front. Now I felt that I had turned into another person. Everything was too big for me so sleeves were rolled up and trouser legs tied up with safety pins but the cap was a perfect fit when my long hair was tucked up under it.

There were five of us in the group: one sister and my brother, and two cousins who had arrived from town that morning to join us, and we were a motley-looking crew kitted out in clothes that were either too big or too small. Our only source of music was a mouth organ which none of us could play properly, but at least it gave us background music, and despite the fact that most of us knew very little about set-dancing we decided that it would be part of our entertainment. The only strong point we had in our repertoire was my brother's singing voice, and even though it would identify us, we felt that we had to capitalise on our one asset. My father had always asserted that wren boys should provide entertainment, so we felt that we should at least make a gallant effort. We decided that we should make a start with the dancing and finish with the song to leave a good parting impression, a bit like the wedding feast at Cana. We had the wind taken out of our sails in one house when the woman of the house announced to her husband that she had never seen dancing quite like ours before. A visitor from London, who was sitting by the fire, remarked that she considered it a bit tribal. It was not a great start, but things got better as we went on and in every house silence descended when my brother started to sing and we knew that we had them. I could see as we went along that he sang different songs in different houses and his choice was always right. In one house where there was an old couple, he sang 'Silent Night' and I could see the old lady's face light up with delight.

'God bless you,' she said, 'that was beautiful.'

By then we were miles from home and I no longer knew the people. 'Who was she?' I asked him when we got outside.

'She taught in our school when I went there first and she taught us "Silent Night".'

'But that must be a long time ago,' I said in surprise.

'It is, but I never forgot her,' he told me. 'She was a real lady.'

It was interesting to go into strange houses and to see the way they had decorated for Christmas, but one farmhouse provided a bit of a shock, for here there was neither tree nor decoration, only a bare candle in a jam-pot on the window. It could have been any ordinary day of the year and I felt very sorry for the children who stood around the kitchen. I had thought that Christmas was important in every house; to find that it was not frightened me a little.

'Why is there no Christmas in that house?' I asked my brother on leaving.

'You're all questions,' he protested.

'But why?' I persisted.

'Because money is more important to them,' he told me, and I sensed that that was all the information I was going to get. But the memory of that bare kitchen stayed with me for the rest of the day.

When we had started collecting in the morning, I had thought that this money was the softest we would ever earn, but as the day wore on I began to have second thoughts. My brother led us across endless fields until I lost all sense of direction. The deep snow slowed our progress, and when we clambered over ditches the snow came down on top of us and some of it found its way down the back of my neck. Jumping off ditches where the snow had drifted against them, we sank deep into it and the effort of continually pulling my legs out of it was exhausting. Apart from the struggle with the snow, my legs also had to contend with the extra burden of trying to set-dance and also to carry clothes that were too large and too heavy. Hunting the wren was not all plain sailing! But the hunger was the biggest problem, and I felt that my stomach and backbone were in close contact. It was getting dark and I was beginning to think that I would never again see home when one of the town cousins produced a bar of chocolate from his pocket. We sat down on the side of a snowy ditch and divided it carefully into five even pieces. I felt as if my life had been saved.

Finally my brother decided that it was time to go home, a decision that I had come to about two hours previously, but because I was only on a test run I had kept my thoughts to myself. As we trudged homewards I ached with tiredness and longed to just lie down and go to sleep, but I followed the others and sometimes my sister came back to give me a pull up a particularly steep field. At last we saw the light of our own house and I almost cried with relief; just a last spurt and we would soon be there.

When we arrived in the door I could smell soup and I had never before smelt anything as good. My mother eased off the heavy, wet clothes; I had not realised what a burden they had been until I was rid of them. Then we sat around the table and she poured hot, thick soup out of a big enamel jug into cups. There was eating and drinking in it, and I told her that it was the most beautiful soup that I ever tasted. She smiled and said, 'Hunger is a great sauce.' After the dinner we counted the takings, and divided by five it was still a sizeable amount, but even the thought of being rich was no substitute for sleep. All I wanted was to get into my bed and sleep. I had discovered that you needed long legs and stamina to go hunting the wren.

from *The Night Before Christmas*
ALICE TAYLOR

THE WREN (THE KING)

Joy, health, love and peace
Be all here in this place
By your leave we will sing
Concerning our King

Our King is well-dressed
In the silks of the best
In ribbons so rare
No King can compare.

We have travelled many miles
Over hedges and stiles
In search of our King
Unto you we bring.

We have powder and shot
To conquer the lot
We have cannon and ball
To conquer them all.

Oh! Christmas is passed
Twelve-tide is the last
So we bid you adieu
Great joy to the New.

Traditional Carol

The popularity of the custom of hunting wrens and robins on Boxing Day drew criticism from some, and this traditional rhyme was an antidote to the Boxing Day revels:

The robin, aye the redbreast,
The robin and the wren,
If ye take out of the nest,
You'll never thrive again.
The robin and the redbreast,
The martin and the swallow,
If you take one of the eggs,
Bad luck will sure to follow.

'SNOW'

The colour of the dawn is lead and white – white snow falling out of a leaden sky to the white earth. The rose branches bend in sharper and sharper curves to the ground, the loaded yew sprays sweet the snow with white plumes. On the sedges the snow is in fleeces; the light strands of clematis are without motion, and have gathered it in clots.

One thrush sings, but cannot long endure the sound of his unchallenged note; the sparrows chirrup in the ricks; the blackbird is waiting for the end of that low tingling noise of the snow falling straight in windless air.

At mid-day the snow is finer, and almost rain, and it begins to pour down from its hives among the branches in short showers or in heavy hovering lumps. The leaves of ivy and holly are gradually exposed in all their gloomy polish, and out bursts the purple of the ash buds and the yellow of new foliage. The beech stems seem in their wetness to be made of a dark agate. Out from their tops blow rags of mist, and not far above them clouds like old spiders' webs go rapidly by.

The snow falls again and the voices of the little summer birds are buried in the silence of the flakes that whirl this way and that aimlessly, rising and falling and crossing or darting horizontally, making the trees sway wearily and their light tops toss and their numbers roar continually in the legions of the wind that whine and moan and shriek their hearts out in the solitary house roofs and doors and round about. The silence of snow co-exists with this roar. One wren pierces it with a needle of song and is gone. The earth and sky are drowning in night and snow.

from *The South Country*
EDWARD THOMAS

UNUSUAL BOXING DAY GAMES AND CUSTOMS

Around 1883 there was an orange custom in Sussex, in which oranges were thrown or bowled along the high roads, and the one whose orange is hit by the orange of another forfeited it to the successful player.

An annual cricket match was played at Newent, in Gloucestershire.

In Scotland, 'sweetie scons' or 'sweetie buns' were presented as gifts, and up to 1827 there was a 'Stephening' custom at Drayton Beauchamp in Bucks when all the villagers used to go to the Rectory to eat bread and cheese and drink ale at the Rector's expense!

At Handsworth, South Yorkshire, in Durham and many parts of the north of England, there is a long tradition of longsword dancing – a style of Morris dancing. Flamborough on the Yorkshire coast, has a longsword dance originating with local fishermen, and this is performed only on Boxing Day outside many pubs in the village.

MUMMER'S PLAYS AND GUISE DANCING

Mummers were a part of every country Christmas until 1914. Their plays of pagan mythology and legends had no scripts but were handed down orally through the generations. Since then only a few have survived: The Paper Boys at Marshfield, near Bristol; at St Alban's, Hertfordshire; at Romsey and Crookham in Hampshire, and in Berkshire. However there have been many revivals throughout the country. Gloucestershire has the Waterley Bottom Mummers from Dursley, and Gloucester, Cheltenham and Stroud each have their own mummers.

In Hampshire they have been revived at Bitterne, Otterbourne, Odiham, and Farnborough. Originally Christmas Eve was the favourite night for the start of Mummers Plays, but over the years this has gradually changed to the morning and lunchtime of Boxing Day. Mumming originates in the masquerades of the Roman Saturnalia festival. The early Christian church endeavoured to give the pagan revels a more spiritual character resulting in the Mysteries or Miracle plays.

Throughout Britain mummers had their own individual names and traditions. At Shoreham in Sussex, they were known as 'Tipteers' or 'Tipteerers'. At Old Basing in Hants, young men called themselves 'The Jolly Christmas Boys' and their play was acted with paper costumes and with music on a tin whistle while in the Lake District, the 'Jolly Boys' ended their play with John Funny asking for money:

Here come I John Funny
I'm the man who collects the money,
It's money we want and money we'll have,
If you don't give us money we'll sweep you all out.

In East Anglia there are remnants of earlier plays at Bottisham, Cambs where boys and men with blackened faces danced to 'rough music' played on pots and pans, and at Thetford in Norfolk with the 'Hummy Dancers.' These were young men who danced in pairs, with one of each pair dressed as a woman. They danced to the music of kettles, saucepans, trays, and a home-made violin, and a feature of the dance was the 'man' beating his 'woman' with a large ladle!

Guise dancing took place in Cornwall and the Scilly Isles right up to Twelfth Night. Bands of people in grotesque costumes used to take to the streets and hold impromptu dances, and some would act out their Christmas plays in the kitchens of the larger houses and farms. The French verb 'to guise' (pronounced 'geeze') means 'to go mumming', and is the origin of the slang term 'old geezer'! Here an old Buckinghamshire mummer shares a memory with Alison Uttley:

'THE MUMMING PLAY'

I met Jack Norris one winter's day and we stood by the eighteenth-century houses in the broad Beaconsfield street talking of this and that. His fingers were bent over the handle of his walking-stick, he leaned towards me with his rosy old face wreathed in smiles.

'D'ye see that cottage over yonder? Just by it, up the entry, there used to be a little school where I learned my lessons. They taught lace-making there in those days.'

I looked across at the tiny old red brick cottage where he and the village children went to school with a dame to teach them.

I asked if he had ever acted in a mumming play, and his face lighted up with the remembrance of it. Indeed he had! He had been dressed up with a lot of others and they had gone all round the public-houses in many a village, singing and acting their play. They began about ten days before Christmas and gave performances every night. They walked miles to give the mumming play.

In comes I,
As light as a Fly.
I've got no money,
And what cares I?

he chanted, and then he laughed with glee at the memory. We stood there, on the pavement, with the cars rushing past and the Army lorries swinging round the green circle, and shoppers hurrying to the grocer's and the fish shop and the bow-windowed chemist's, and he told me of other days, evoking the past so that I felt that these people around us were phantoms of the future.

'There's one as went a-mumming with me,' he cried, pointing with his stick across the wide street. Up the road, under the shadow of the black and white timbered Saracen's Head, came a bent old man wearing a greatcoat, stumbling along with his staff. He might have been brought from another era of time, he looked like Father Time himself as he moved along, unconscious of our gaze. We stood and watched him as he rounded the corner with the painted Saracen above him, as he walked with tottering steps past the courtyard entrance, past many windows, towards the little cottages.

'And there's another as went with us,' cried my companion, and we saw a second figure come up the long road and wander past the Saracen's Head. I felt we were conjuring up something from the deep past; I felt that in another moment snow would fall and a coach and four would clatter up the Wycombe End from Oxford, and cloaked and hooded figures would descend at the door of the famous hostelry. The ostler would run out, the stable doors would open, fresh horses would be led into

the yard, and the heavily cloaked coachman would perhaps wind his long horn. I thought that the band of mummers would come round the corner of the Saracen's Head, dressed in their motley, with ribbons fluttering and drums beating and pipe playing, and children running after.

'I'll come and act the play for you, ma'am, if you like,' said the old man. 'I remembers it all.' So it was agreed.

Every year the mummers went round the villages at Christmas time, acting their play. In many counties there were different versions of the mumming play, but probably each parish varied the play to suit the actors. The simple plot of the play, which was the same throughout the whole of England, showed that it had a common origin. There was a fight between two characters, one of whom was a soldier. A man was 'slain,' and the doctor was called in. The slain man was miraculously cured with a bottle or a pill. I remember a version we acted in our home when we were children, where the doctor held out a black bottle to the fallen St George, saying:

Take a little out of my bottle,
And pour it down thy throttle,
Then rise up, Bold Slasher,
And fight again,

and we draped antimacassars around our heads and fought again.

All the characters vary. Sometimes there is St George, or the Duke of Cumberland, or King George. There are soldiers and odd strange people to give a part to many. A man dressed up as a woman was an integral part of this mumming play. All the faces were blacked for disguise. The costumes were of the simplest kind: a top hat, a soldier's helmet, cut paper frills and streamers pinned to jackets and waistcoats, dangling ribbons of bright colours. The swords borne by the fighters were wooden laths with cross-pieces or walking-sticks, and sometimes a real sword.

The characters were announced by one of the actors who entered first. So Jack Norris acted the play for me, and I wrote down his words as he declaimed them and sang them, and laughed over them. He came knocking at my door, and I opened it as if I lived at the inn. He hobbled in and did his part most valiantly.

This version of the play was acted at Beaconsfield and Wooburn and neighbouring villages. Many hamlets were visited, and they finished up at Wooburn Green.

The mummers stood outside the door of the inn and one character, Hi Down Derry, knocked loudly and pushed the door open and called:

'Please remember the mummers!'

This warned the company that a performance was about to take place, and the people at the inn prepared for the mummers.

from *Buckinghamshire*
ALISON UTTLEY

Country writer H. J. Massingham shares with us an old mummers' night recipe from Chipping Campden in the Cotswolds:

I wound up mummers' night by extracting the recipe of the rum punch which was served hot in a leathern cauldron with a long ladle. The nucleus of the heady brew was a gallon of ale, kept simmering on the fire. To this were added sugar, cinnamon, nutmeg and spice, and into the steaming compost poured a bottle of whisky, one of old brandy, one of rum and one of sherry. These were to give a little life to it. Then, just for bite and tang, a bottle of Cointreau and another of Benedictine were emptied into a pot seething with potential life-giving qualities like the primaeval ooze. It was a great moment when the mystic brew was brought into the circle of expectant faces. Nobody remarked the arrival of the posset, nobody discontinued his affabilities to his neighbour or the company. But a gleam in the eye, a stiffening in the seated manner, a forced note in the conversation and a something distrait in the responses, made me aware that the ladle was in for many a journey between mug and cauldron.

from *Wold Without End*
H. J. MASSINGHAM

PANTOMIME

Boxing Day is traditionally the starting day for Pantomime. Its origins can be traced back to the great court masques and the mummers plays. The first pantomime was performed in 1717 and it gradually became a fairy-tale fantasy for all the family, with dancing, topical jokes, and transformation scenes. The tradition of a masculine dame and a female principal boy harks back to the days of the Roman Saturnalia and the topsy-turvey world of Misrule.

The 26 December also is a time for more festivities and celebrations, but few today could ever emulate the old country feasts. In the next extract Sir Jonah Barrington remembers a St Stephen's Day Banquet in Ireland with particular relish.

MUMMERS' JIG

Music: P. Burgess ©

The Christmas custom of performing the Mummers play, often included songs and dance. The songs varied considerably, but were usually something popular at the time and acted as greater inducement for spectators to dip into their pockets. The dances either had links with Morris dances, or were solo dances for individual characters. Some Irish performances featured several musicians, who would perform a wide repertoire of tunes as part of the entertainment. This tune was written by Paul Burgess.

Close to the kennel of his hounds my father had built a small cottage which was occupied solely by an old huntsman, his older wife, and his nephew, a whipper-in. The chase, and the bottle, and the piper were the enjoyments of winter, and nothing could recompense a suspension of these enjoyments.

My elder brother justly apprehending that the frost and snow of Christmas might probably prevent their usual occupation of the chase, determined to provide against any listlessness during the shut-up period by an uninterrupted match of what was called 'hard-going' till the weather should break up.

A hogshead of superior claret was, therefore, sent to the cottage of old Quin, the huntsman; and a fat cow, killed and plundered of her skin, was hung up by the heels. All the windows were closed to keep out the light. One room, filled with straw and numerous blankets, was destined for a bed-chamber in common, and another was prepared as a kitchen for the use of the servants. Claret, cold, mulled, or buttered, was to be the beverage for the whole company, and in addition to the cow above mentioned, chickens, bacon and bread were the only admitted viands. Wallace and Hosey, my father's and brother's pipers, and Boyle, a blind but a famous fiddler, were employed to enliven the banquet, which it was determined should continue till the cow became a skeleton, and the claret should be on its stoop . . .

As for myself, I was too unseasoned to go through more than the first ordeal, which was on a frosty St Stephen's Day, when the 'hard-goers' partook of their opening banquet, and several neighbours were invited, to honour the commencement of what they called their 'shut-up pilgrimage.'

The old huntsman was the only male attendant, and his ancient spouse, once a kitchen-maid in the family, now somewhat resembling the amiable Leonarda in Gil Blas, was the cook, whilst the drudgery fell to the lot of the whipper-in. A long knife was prepared to cut collops from the cow; a large turf fire seemed to court the gridiron; the pot bubbled up as if proud of its contents, whilst plump white chickens floated in crowds upon the surface of the water; the simmering potatoes, just burst-

ing their drab surtouts, exposed the delicate whiteness of their mealy bosoms; the claret was tapped, and the long earthen wide-mouthed pitchers stood gaping under the impatient cock, to receive their portions. The pipers plied their chants, the fiddler tuned his Cremona, and never did any feast commence with more auspicious appearances of hilarity and dissipation, appearances which were not doomed to be falsified.

I shall never forget the attraction this novelty had for my youthful mind. All thoughts but those of good cheer were for the time totally obliterated. A few curses were, it is true, requisite to spur on old Leonarda's skill, but at length the banquet entered: the luscious smoked bacon, bedded in its cabbage mattress, and partly obscured by its own savoury steam, might have tempted the most fastidious of epicures; whilst the round trussed chickens, ranked by the half dozen on hot pewter dishes, turned up their white plump merry-thoughts, exciting equally the eye and appetite; fat collops of the hanging cow, sliced indiscriminately from her tenderest points, grilled over the clear embers upon a shining gridiron, half-drowned in their own luscious juices, and garnished with little pyramids of congenial shallots, smoked at the bottom of the well-furnished board. A prologue of cherry-bounce (brandy) preceded the entertainment, which was enlivened by hob-nobs and joyous toasts.

Numerous toasts, in fact, as was customary in those days, intervened to prolong and give zest to the repast – every man shouted forth his fair favourite, or convivial pledge; and each voluntarily surrendered a portion of his own reason in bumpers to the beauty of his neighbour's toast. The pipers jerked from their bags appropriate planxties to every jolly sentiment; the jokers cracked the usual jests and ribaldry; one songster chanted the joys of wine and women; another gave, in full glee, the pleasures of the fox chase; the fiddler sawed his merriest jigs; the old huntsman sounded his horn, and thrusting his forefingers into his ear, to aid the quaver, gave the view halloa! of nearly ten minutes' duration, to which melody tally ho! was responded by every stentorian voice. A fox's brush stuck into a candlestick, in the centre of the tables, was worshipped as a divinity! Claret flowed, bumpers

were multiplied, and chickens, in the garb of spicy spitchcocks, assumed the name of devils to whet the appetites which it was impossible to conquer!

My reason gradually began to lighten me of its burden, and in its last efforts kindly suggested the straw-chamber as my asylum. Two couple of favourite hounds had been introduced to share in the joyous pastime of their friends and master; and the deep bass of their throats, excited by the shrillness of the huntsman's tenor, harmonised by two rattling pipers, a jiggling fiddler, and twelve voices, in twelve different keys, all bellowing in one continuous unrelenting chime, was the last point of recognition which Bacchus permitted me to exercise, for my eyes began to perceive a much larger company than the room actually contained; the lights were more than doubled, without any virtual increase of their number, and even the chairs and tables commenced dancing a series of minuets before me. A faint tally ho! was attempted by my reluctant lips; but I believe the effort was unsuccessful, and I very soon lost, in the straw-room, all that brilliant consciousness of existence in the possession of which the morning had found me so happy.

Just as I was closing my eyes to a twelve hours' slumber, I distinguished the general roar of 'stole away!' which rose almost up to the very roof of old Quin's cottage.

At noon, next day, a scene of a different nature was exhibited. I found, on waking, two associates by my side, in as perfect insensibility as that from which I had just aroused. Our piper seemed indubitably dead! but the fiddler, who had the privilege of age and blindness, had taken a hearty nap, and seemed as much alive as ever.

The room of banquet had been re-arranged by the old woman; spitchcocked chickens, fried rashers, and broiled marrow-bones appeared struggling for precedence. The clean cloth looked itself fresh and exciting; jugs of mulled and buttered claret foamed hot upon the re-furnished table, and a better or heartier breakfast I never in my life enjoyed.

A few members of the jovial crew had remained all night at their posts, but, I suppose, alternately took some rest, as they seemed not at all affected by their repletion…

Fresh visitors were introduced each successive day, and the seventh morning had arisen before the feast broke up. As that day advanced, the cow was proclaimed to have furnished her full quantum of good dishes; the claret was upon its stoop, and the last gallon, mulled with a pound of spices, was drunk in tumblers to the next merry meeting! All now retired to their natural rest, until the evening announced a different scene.

An early supper, to be partaken of by all the young folks of both sexes in the neighbourhood, was provided in the dwelling-house to terminate the festivities. A dance, as usual, wound up the entertainment, and what was then termed a 'raking pot of tea' put a finishing stroke, in jollity and good humour, to such a revel as I never saw before, and, I am sure, shall never see again.

Sir Jonah Barrington (1760–1834) from *A Book of Ireland*
FRANK O'CONNOR

27 DECEMBER ST JOHN'S DAY

The Feast of St John, where celebrated is a day for visiting friends. The tradesmen of Driffield in Yorkshire were the first in the county to observe the 27 December as a holiday – 'to allow those in

Drive the Cold Winter Away

Words: Trad./Music: J. Coppin/J. Broomhall. ©

1. All hail to the days that mer-it more praise Than all the rest of the year And wel-come the nights that dou-ble de-lights As well for the poor as the peer! Good for-tune att-end each mer-ry man's friend That does the best that he may, For-get-ting all wrongs with car-ols and songs, To drive the cold win-ter a-way.

CHORUS

A - way, A- way, to drive the cold win-ter a-way, For-get-ting all wrongs with car-ols and songs, To drive the cold win-ter a- way.

2. 'Tis ill for a mind to anger inclined
   To think of small injuries now;
   If wrath be to seek, do not lend her your cheek,
   Nor let her inhabit your brow.
   Cross out of your books malevolent looks,
   Both beauty and youth's decay,
   And wholly consort with laughter and sport,
   To drive the cold winter away.

CH: *Away, Away, to drive the cold winter away.*
    And wholly consort with laughter and sport,
    To drive the cold winter away.

3. This time of the year is spent in good cheer,
   And neighbours together do meet,
   To sit by the fire, with friendly desire,
   Each other in love to greet.
   Old grudges forgot are put in the pot,
   All sorrows aside they lay;
   The old and the young all carol this song,
   To drive the cold winter away . . .

CH: *Away, Away, to drive the cold winter away.*
    The old and the young all carol this song,
    To drive the cold winter away.

Three verses of an old song with timeless sentiments set to a new tune. The first two verses are by Tom Durfey (1653–1723), the dramatist and friend of Charles II, and were published in his Pills to Purge Melancholy *of 1719. A version of the whole song is in the Pepysian Collection.*

their employ the opportunity of visiting distant friends.'

At Uttoxeter in Staffordshire up to around 1913 there used to be a Hiring Fair. In Scotland the days between Christmas and Hogmanay were known as 'Daft Days,' and Daft Days Yule Bread – a thin oatmeal loaf with a sign of the cross marked on it – was made. On St John's Day in Germany it was thought lucky to drink large quantities of wine that had been blessed by the local priest, while in Austria, drinking the blessed wine was a safeguard against being struck by lightning. As if they needed any excuse!

For some the 27 December is the time to reflect on and record the Christmas celebrations. Here is an entry from the diary of Anne Hughes, a Herefordshire farmer's wife of the late eighteenth century:

'The Diary of a Farmer's Wife' 1796–1797

Dec. ye 27. Christmas be all over now, and our visitors gone, but a right good time we did have, the roads did dry up a bit so not too bad for the travellers, who did cum pack horse. Cusson Tom and Emma, her ladd and his sweetheart Jan, did get here after a journie of hard going Christmas Eve, the rest did cum Christmas morning and all of us to church leaving carters wiffe and Sarahs sister Jane to help Sarah with the dinner to be all ready genst our cumming back, and mother and me did set the tables together in a row and cover them with my linnen table cloths; then we did put the silver and glass and all did look verrie fine. Passon did give a verrie good sermon, telling us to do to others as we would have them do to us, and the world the better place, to which I do agree. The singing did go right heartilie with a great roar, the church bein full, for all do like the young passon and his mother.

Then we out and home to our dinner. John did set at one end with beef and geese, and Farmer Ellis at the other to cut up the hams and so on, which Sarah and Jane did

carry round till all served, and all did eat their fill and had plentie. Then John did pass the wine and all did drink each other's healths; then the men did smoke while we ladies did drink our wine and talk of divers things that had happened through the year, not thinking so much had; then the men did say let us dance, so Bill and Jen did play a merrie jig on their fiddles and we did step it out finely; till all breathless, we do sit down laffing much.

28 December: Holy Innocents' Day (or Childermas)

As this commemorated King Herod's massacre of the children, it was universally believed to be a very unlucky day. In particular it was thought very unlucky to marry, do any housework, transact any business, travel (especially by sea), wear new clothes, cut one's nails, or wash any clothes on this day.

In Northumberland, lead miners would not enter the mine on Innocents' Day.

In Northamptonshire the 28th was known as 'Dyzemas day,' and in Shropshire 'Cross day' – they applied this name also throughout the year to the day of the week on which it had last fallen. This day of the week was then also widely believed to be unlucky for starting any work or undertaking, hence the saying 'It must have been begun on Cross day.'

In many churches, a muffled peal of bells was rung, and this custom survived at Woodchester, in Gloucestershire until the 1960s.

This was the last day of the Boy bishop's reign. On his last day of office he went in procession through the town to bless the assembled people. A special dinner was held, and he had to preach a sermon. This old custom did not last beyond the reign of Mary I in Britain, and the eighteenth century in the rest of Europe, but it was revived in some English parish churches in a modified way, without the boy bishops having to take services or preach.

In some areas there were indulgences for children. In the Preston area of Lancs. in the 1870s, it was thought an appropriate day for children's parties and treats, while at Exton in Rutland and in parts of Gloucestershire, children were allowed to play in the church. In Derbyshire, children often playfully gave each other 'a good hiding' because it was Childermas.

29 AND 30 DECEMBER

Hiring Fairs called 'Giglet Fairs' (or 'Giglot Fairs') were common in Cornwall, Devon, and other South Western counties in the week after Christmas. Everyone was free to speak to one of the opposite sex without the formality of an introduction, and without chaperones! Men and maids could become 'tokened,' by sealing their match with a token – a brooch or tie pin.

Cornish writer Mollie Bartlett has this memory:

'I have heard my granny tell the story of a farm-maid who got tokened to the chap of her choice, and she bought him a pair of cuff-links. In return the young man asked to see a card of brooches, which were marked at twopence each. After a very careful inspection he asked the shopkeeper if he had any penny ones! Whereupon the 'tokening' was called off by the maid!'

INNOCENT'S SONG

Words: Charles Causley/Music: J. Coppin ©

1. Who's that knock - ing on the win - dow,
Who's that knock-ing on the door, What are all those pres-ents
ly-ing on the kitch-en floor? Who is the smi-ling stra-nger with his
hair as white as gin, What is he doing with the chil-dren Who
could have let him in? *Why has he rub- ies on his fing- ers,*
A cold, cold crown on his head, *Why, when he caws his*

car - ol, Does the salt - y snow run red?

2. Why does he ferry my fireside
    As a spider on a thread,
    His fingers made of fuses
    And his tongue of gingerbread?
    Why does the world before him
    Melt in a million suns,
    Why do his yellow, yearning eyes
    Burn like saffron buns?

CH. *Watch where he comes walking*
    Out of the Christmas flame,
    Dancing, double talking:
    Herod is his name.

Another poem from Charles Causley, here showing his gift for powerful imagery and the influence of popular song and ballad form. A joy to set to music and a joy to sing.

The days leading up to New Year is also the time for ghost stories and for writing those thank-you letters! I can't resist including this poem from Mick Gowar:

CHRISTMAS THANK YOU'S

Dear Auntie
Oh, what a nice jumper
I've always adored powder blue
and fancy you thinking of
orange and pink
for the stripes
how clever of you!

Dear Uncle
The soap is
terrific
So
useful
and such a kind thought and
how did you guess that
I'd just used the last of
the soap that last Christmas brought

Dear Gran
Many thanks for the hankies
Now I really can't wait for the flu
and the daisies embroidered
in red round the 'M'
for Michael
how
thoughtful of you!

Dear Cousin
What socks!
and the same sort you wear
so you must be
the last word in style
and I'm certain you're right that the
luminous green
will make me stand out a mile

Dear Sister
I quite understand your concern
it's a risk sending jam in the post
But I think I've pulled out
all the big bits
of glass
so it won't taste too sharp
spread on toast

Dear Grandad
Don't fret
I'm delighted
So don't think your gift will
offend
I'm not at all hurt
that you gave up this year
and just sent me
a fiver
to spend

MICK GOWAR

NEW YEAR

'Love and Joy come to you
And to you your Wassail too,
And God Bless You and Send you a Happy New Year
And God send you a Happy New Year.'

NEW YEAR'S EVE OR HOGMANAY

Almost all customs and traditions associated with New Year are of pagan origin.

Hogmanay is the most important festival in Scotland with communal parties held in streets, houses and village halls. The many customs include 'First footing,' the 'Hide of the Bag,' the haggis, the *Caise Calluinn* (or Christmas Cheese), and the New Year's Blessing. Before the New Year can be welcomed, all the evil and bad luck of the old year must be banished or driven away. Sometimes this was loaded on to scapegoats such as cats or dogs, and then driven from the home, and sometimes this was driven away with noise as in the *Caisean a 'Bhuilg* (or 'Hide of the Bag') tradition in the Scottish Highlands. This ancient ritual was performed at night by the *gillean Callaig* or 'Hogmanay Lads.' One was covered with the hide of a bull to which the horns and hooves were still attached, and with the other boys beating the hide with sticks, they would run round houses three times in a sunwise direction. They would also beat the walls of houses and chant Hogmanay rhymes, all designed to keep at bay evil spirits and hostile forces of every kind. One of these began:

> *Hogmanay of the sack,*
> *Hogmanay of the sack,*
> *Strike the hide,*
> *Strike the hide.*
> *Hogmanay of the sack,*
> *Hogmanay of the sack,*
> *Beat the skin,*
> *Beat the skin . . .*

In some areas the hide was singed by the man of the house, as the fumes it gave off were believed to have powers of purification and bring health to all the family in the coming year. In some rituals the breast-skin of a sheep, goat or deer was wrapped round the point of a shinty stick, and this was singed in the fire.

In some parts of Scotland, juniper was burned in the house to protect all the family and the animals from harm. It was also very important to drive stray dogs away because of their association with evil, although these were mild compared with the spirit-hounds who roamed much of Britain and the Celtic lands. They are particularly active in Wales on New Year's Eve, when the '*Cwn Annwn*' are celebrated as spirit-hounds passing through the air. Their howling is regarded as an omen of death, and the dogs appear in a variety of forms. Sometimes they are white and small with tiny ears, sometimes black and very ugly with huge red spots. But most terrible of all are those of a blood-red colour, dripping with gore, and with eyes like balls of liquid fire!

The Nordic theme of these demon dogs is particularly strong in the north, and well illustrated by the ghost story of the Druggan Hill Dog in Cumbria:

As usual with most ghosts no hard dates are given; we are simply told that many decades ago, or once upon a time, a pedlar who travelled the Plumbland district suddenly disappeared at Druggan Hill and the local community suspected that he had been murdered for the value of his pack and his body buried in a nearby quarry. From the time when this pedlar vanished there appeared a strange, large black dog which for the next twenty years frequented the Druggan Hill neigh-

bourhood; this was popularly supposed to be the spirit of the vanished pedlar and was named the 'Druggan Hill Boggle'.

One cold winter's night the owner of the last house at the Plumbland end of Parnsonby heard loud thudding sounds at the front gate and groaning. At length he summoned the courage to look out and found a neighbour, Joseph Dobieson, lying on the doorstep in a collapsed condition and with his left hand badly lacerated. He was taken indoors and recovered sufficiently to give an account of what had happened to him: at the stile at the foot of Druggan Hill he had fallen over a large black dog which had slunk after him, filling him with dread, so that at last he had turned on the animal to confront it with

the cry, 'Tha must be t'Druggan Hill boggle!' Whereat his hand had split open and the dog vanished into thin air (a suggested alternative version is that the dog bit him because he scared it and then it ran away). Dobieson's injured hand refused to heal.

In the course of time, during work at the quarry, there was unearthed the skeleton of a man buried in a doubled position; the suspected remains of the pedlar. These were removed to the churchyard for burial and from that time the black dog was never seen again. Moreover, Dobieson's hand was miraculously healed.

from *Cumberland Heritage*
by Molly Lefebure

THE OLD YEAR

The Old Year's gone away
To nothingness and night:
We cannot find him all the day
Nor hear him in the night:
He left no footstep, mark or place
In either shade or sun:
The last year he'd a neighbour's face,
In this he's known by none.

All nothing everywhere:
Mists we on mornings see
Have more of substance when they're here
And more of form than he.
He was a friend by every fire,
In every cot and hall –
A guest to every heart's desire,
And now he's nought at all.

Old papers thrown away,
Old garments cast aside,
The talk of yesterday,
All things identified;
But times once torn away
No voices can recall:
The eve of New Year's Day
Left the Old Year lost to all.

JOHN CLARE

FIRST-FOOTING

First-footing is still widely practised. Once midnight has struck, a dark-haired man should be the first person to cross your threshold. He traditionally brings a small lump of coal or peat which he throws into the fire to bring good luck, and maintain a link with ancient fire rituals. The 'first-footer' was sometimes called the 'boy visitor', and also known as a 'lucky bird' in Durham and Yorkshire.

'Letting in Christmas' was much more of a northern custom. It was customary to give the first-footers cake and wine, and some dark-haired boys even earned a lot of money. In Shropshire and many parts of the country it was considered bad luck for a woman or a red-haired man to be the first comer on New Year's Day, so it was quite common for dark-haired young men or boys to be employed to pay an early visit!

In Herefordshire they used to open the back door to let the old year out, and then the front door to let the New Year in. In Clun in Shropshire old families used to let a man in at the back door and then out the front. An old man at Longnor always entered the house without knocking or speaking and silently stirred the fire with a poker before greeting the family. This was also recorded at Caistor in Lincolnshire and is a ceremony that perhaps stems from earlier Midwinter fire worship.

At Skipsea in Holderness, Lincolnshire, young men used to blacken their faces, wear disguises and go round chalking up the date of the new year on gates, doors and shutters. No-one stopped them as it was considered very lucky to have a house 'dated'.

In parts of Scotland young men in disguise would call at the kitchens of the larger houses and farms to claim the right to kiss every unmarried woman in the room. It was also a time for practical jokes and Misrule; during the night parts of fishing-boats and carts were hidden or doors blocked to prevent any work next day.

There's an old Colliery Custom in Northumberland called 'Bussin-the-tup' or 'Dressing the tup.' The tup was the last skip of coal drawn from the pit on New Year's Eve, and this was decorated with lighted candles.

Processions of various kinds were once a major feature of New Year's Eve. In the Orkneys it was customary for a large group of people to process round the parish, knock on every door and sing a song that begins:

This night is guid New'r E'en's night,
We're a' here Queen Mary's men;
And we're come here to crave our right,
And that's before our Lady . . .

On the Island of Guernsey, children used to dress up a figure in the shape of a man, and after parading it through the streets, bury it on the sea-shore. The ceremony was called *enterrer le vieux bout de l'an* (to bury the old end of the year). Processions have survived in a few places; they originate from pagan fire rituals to ward off evil. At the Tar Barrel Procession at Allendale, Northumberland, young men burn the old year out by carrying blazing tar barrels on their heads, and at midnight they throw the barrels into a bonfire and dance round it. At Comrie on Tayside there is a traditional 'Flambeaux' or torchlight procession; at Stonehaven in Grampian men swing balls of rags and tar through the town to the accompaniment of a pipe band; and at Biggar in Lanarkshire, they burn out the old year with a large bonfire at the town cross.

BELL-RINGING

Everywhere bells are rung to mark the start of the year. Sometimes a muffled peal was rung first for the old year, then on the last stroke of midnight the bells rang out an open peal for the new year. This tradition continues at Cirencester in Gloucestershire. At Over in Cambridgeshire, the bellringers held their annual supper on New Year's Eve at the Swan Inn. They ate roast beef and drank 'Hot pot' – a mixture of beer, spirits, eggs, milk, sugar, and nutmeg in a cowhorn known as a 'Long Tot' or a 'Long Tom'. In Dorset, the bells of Milton Abbey are said to ring under water on New Year's Eve. It is thought that Lord Milton had them removed because they once seemed to be celebrating his departure for London.

Writing from under Bredon Hill in Worcestershire, Fred Archer recalls an historic occasion for the village bellringers:

'NEW YEAR, 1900'

Ashton Bellringers, all five of them, looked thoughtfully at the dying embers in the schoolroom grate. This was the very last supper for them in the century. The village women had cleared and washed up the crocks, Dr Overthrow, who had been chairman once more, had gone home to sit the old year out and the new year in.

'Another hour and it ull be nineteen hundred,' said John Stallard, Captain of Ashton's Church Tower.

'Oi and the old Queen's still on the throne,' spoke up young Jim Bowman. 'Good 'ooman her a bin, our old man rung the treble bell, same as I does, at the Coronation.'

The nine-gallon barrel, trammed and tapped in the corner of the schoolroom, just dribbled another mugful for Jim Bowman's brother, George.

'He's a getting low,' Joe Bradfield belched, 'like the year, oi and the century – almost gone. Pack a feow writing slates a' the backside on him, I can do with another pint; 'tis like the tay pot – some a the best's in the bottom,' and with this Frank Wheatcroft helped Joe to tilt the barrel. Nothing stirred in Ashton School after the last dregs had been drained from the barrel; there was just the monotonous tick tick of the clock, the wheeze of pipe lighting as a pall of blue tobacco smoke rose to the rafters.

Then John Stallard spoke, 'Now then, you chaps, look lissom, it only wants twenty-five minutes to twelve.' As the men rose to walk down the road to the church the chill night air penetrated their thick cord trousers. Soon they were in the belfry. By lantern light, like their fathers before them, five men stood in a little circle. At John's signal the sally end of the rope was grasped and away

went the team. One, two, three, four, five. A merry peal, the last merry peal of the nineteenth century. Nods from John again at ten to twelve; ringing stopped while up among the woodwork and the furrowed wheels where ropes had worn themselves out time and time again, the bells stood green and cold.

'Look slippy, Jim, we an't got all night, bring up the leather mufflers.'

These were fixed in position to muffle the sound of the bells as the old year departed. 'Mufflers in position,' John reported. 'Now for the Buff Peal as we calls it. Mind they be only half muffled.'

The ringing began again, ding, dong, ding, dong, ding. Balm, Balm, Balm, Balm, Balm, the death of the year and the century.

'It's sad mind, five more minutes according to the clock in the ringing chambers,' John shouted above the noise of the bells.

Jim Bowman's thoughts wandered to his father ringing for the Queen's Coronation and how the five Ashton men had rung for two Jubilees. The Queen could not live much longer. Then another Coronation, a king this time. The minutes ticked by until twelve when that pause the villagers waited for arrived.

'Happy New Year,' John said for one and all, 'and let's have them mufflers off. Now for some ringing, you chaps.'

George grabbed his sally. 'Pity we a only got five bells, if we had six we ud ring a peal to be sure.'

'Fire um!' ordered John, and like one man five ringers pulled together and all the bells rang out over the countryside like cannon in battle. 'Keep firing um, we shan't see the end a the nineteen hundreds.'

Blowings now, while the rum Millie Bostock had left for them was equalled out.

'Next time,' John shouted, and away went the bells, sadly end of ropes being pulled and loosed as their red and white ebbed and flowed like a tide.

'Remember when Harry Hill never loosed his sally, went up on the rope with the tenor, then let go just afore his brains ud a bin knocked out on the ceiling? Oi, that was the Jubilee of '87,' John told George.

The other men looked at the clock. It was twenty past twelve.

'What about it, chaps?' Jim said. 'I a got to milk master Jinks's cows in the morning.'

The bells were stilled. Once more the men took the night air, this time to the village cross. Here they stood around their lanterns, hung on a bean pole pushed securely in the turf, to sing their carol to the new year, the new century.

> *Arise ye sleep-y souls a - - - rise!*
> *Take your mor-ning Sac-ri-fice;*
> *Laud and mag-ni-fy the Name*
> *Of our Great Redeemer's fame!*

This was a traditional welcome to the New Year, handed down from father to son. As the fourth verse ended, Millie

Bostock came from her cottage, inviting the men to walk through to bring her luck. A tall dark man first, Frank Wheatcroft was the man. Here, on the threshold of the new year, Millie poured port wine into dainty glasses, served mince pies on the little mahogany table in front of a roaring fire. Warmed by the fire, by the wine, Millie asked for just one carol in her front room.

'Christmas is come and gone, Miss Bostock,' George Bowman said, 'But we can sing "All Hail and Praise", same as we sung yer Boxing Night.'

Millie knew they would and had the page turned ready in her music book to accompany them on the piano. In the early hours of January 1st the little party went to their cottages, having once more said farewell to one year and welcomed another. As Millie turned down the wick in her front-room lamp and went to bed she prayed the dark man would bring her luck.

from *The Secrets of Bredon Hill*
FRED ARCHER

CAKES

In Scotland there is a strong tradition of children begging for cakes or bread. Sir Walter Scott described how a hundred children danced to the pipes and received a piece of cake and bannock and pennies in honour of hogmanay. Often there were rhymes and chants like 'Hogmanay, Trollolay, give us of your white bread and none of your grey,' and my favourite and more to the point: 'My feet's cauld, my shoon's thin; gie's my cakes, and let me in!'

In Northumberland and Scotland 'hogmanay' was the name of a small cake given to children or to spice bread and cheese given away at New Year.

In Shropshire caraway buns were dipped in ale and known as 'wigs', while in the West of Scotland, oat bannocks flavoured with caraway seeds were baked. One was made for every child in the house on Hogmanay evening, and if one broke in the baking, it foretold misfortune to the owner in the coming year.

SUPERSTITIONS

In the 1950s a farmer at Queenhill, Upton-on-Severn, Worcestershire always took all his loose money out of his pocket, laid it on the grass in front of his house, and left it there all night to bring good luck in the New Year. In Scotland they left the smallest silver coin on the doorstep. If it was missing in the morning then it would be poverty next year; and prosperity if it was left untouched!

It was thought unlucky to continue the knitting of a stocking into the New Year.

In Herefordshire, a mistletoe bough was cut on New Year's Eve and hung up in a stall at the stroke of midnight. At the same time the old mistletoe bough was taken down and burnt.

'Joseph was a tinner' was a common saying in both Cornwall and Somerset. St Joseph of Arimathea traded in Cornish tin and Somerset lead, and this song was sung by gypsy mummers in the early 1900s:

Here come Three Josephs, Three Josephs are here,
All for to bring 'ee the Luck of the Year.
One he did stand at the Babe's right hand,
One was a lord in Egypt's land,
One was a tinner and sailed the sea.
God keep you merry, say we.

God bless the cattle, the corn and hay,
And the skill of your timber and tools alway,
And God send the workers good metal and free.
God keep you merry, say we.

Severnside fisherman had a rhyme: 'Joseph was a tinner, a-sailing on the sea. God bless the fishing, and God bless me.'

The Legend of the Fairies Song at Hogmanay in the Hebrides was as follows.

Donald was a hump-backed man on his way to Scalasaig to buy New Year provisions. On passing a green knoll above Killoran Bay, he came upon a group of fairies dancing to a rhyme based on the days of the week. He had a good ear for music and knew there was something out of time with the tune. The fairies had forgotten the Gaelic name for Wednesday – so Donald chimed in with '*Di-ceu-daoin*' which made all the difference. At the end of the dance, the hillock opened and the fairies disappeared taking Donald with them. They held him for a year and a day, and to reward him, removed his hump, and sent him back to the world a straight-backed man.

WEATHER-LORE

If New Year's Eve night-wind blows south
It betokeneth warmth and growth;
If west, much milk, and fish in the sea;
If north, cold and storms there will be:
If east, the trees will bear much fruit;
If north-east, flee it, man and brute!

The importance of the Hogmanay celebrations in Scotland is captured wonderfully in this extract by M. O'Donoghue:

The year's last day was papered in black, with the dark giving way to a gloaming for only a few hours. We were so far north that we had to light our way through the winters with candles and lived like pit ponies for four months of the year.

But, in this long night, there was hoarding and scrimping and the clonking of secret full bottles and the whiffs of midnight baking. To be run short of anything on Hogmanay would have been unthinkable. We had no Christmas puddings, but the black bread was richer and fruitier than a brandy-soaked squire and the shortbread dissolved into sweet, crumbly butter on our tongues.

All day was an impatient hunt for things to do until evening. The girls pressed their dresses a dozen times and Granny Morag and Annie rummaged for old cups and mugs and jam-jars, anything that would serve for the hospitality.

We boys, evicted from the domestic scene, met others to push and loaf with, aimlessly hovering round the harvour or hacking branches off trees with our knives, until it was time to go home and put on our kilts.

At eight o'clock Robbie beag arrived with his woman, Siubhan, and Bert from the farm with his father, and all the tinkers from next door. Even grim Uncle Tómas came with Alice at his heels, blushing and giggling over his once-a-year good nature, and our cousins almost relaxed. The cottage was so full that the walls seemed to bulge and people continually fell backwards over the fender and burnt their bottoms on the range.

Our Uncle Angus and Bert's Da tucked their fiddles under their chins and sawed away like two manic Pied Pipers in a personal struggle that went back to before anyone else in the room was born. They refused to stand together, so pulled us from one end of the kitchen to the other with their music and glowered at each other through the gaps in the crowd. It was generally agreed that Bert's Da had the technique, but auld Angus had the heart.

And, as we buried the old year, memories and regrets and secret vows and hopes joined the wake and the very young grew excited about the new tomorrow and our older brothers and sisters began to exchange long, candy looks and the parents and grandparents and uncles and aunts and friends remembered the years spent together before and welcomed the coming one to them. Good and bad, we loved each other deeply and the mid-night chimes began to strike.

One . . . two . . . three . . . four . . . and Robbie beag was pushed hastily out of the back door . . . five . . . six . . . seven . . . eight . . . and everyone began kissing every one else . . . nine . . . ten . . . eleven . . . last second of the old year, first instant of the new . . . twelve! A Happy New Year! A Happy New Year!

The back door was shaking under the pounding from outside and Granny Morag flung it wide open to let our 'first foot' in. Dark and handsome, our Uncle Robbie beag crossed the threshold with his magic gifts for the New Year; a lump of coal to bring us warmth, a piece of black bun to bring us food, a farthing for prosperity and a smoked herring, dressed in coloured crêpe paper, for luck; and a bottle.

Granny Morag took a respectable sook from that and revived her son with a bottle of her own whisky, as he was pulled joyously to the fire.

We sang 'Auld Lang Syne' and the women wiped their eyes and filled the glasses till our throats scorched and Auntie Annie got so carried away that she sang an unrhythmical solo in a forgotten, quavering voice and burst into tears at the end when everyone applauded.

Then it was our turn to go first-footing and we fell gasping from the pupa of bodies into the night pool, blowing bubbles which rose to the sky as wraiths; swept along by the wind, as cold on the outside as if we were naked, but with a whisky lining which kept us from caring. Snowflakes wriggled in our ears like tadpoles and slid over the tops of our gumboots, rubbing raw patches on our calves and trickling down the insides till our toes chattered.

Others passed us in single file, black lumps behind a lantern, on the way to our cottage and the farm and Drew Heggie at the Slaughter.

'A guid Hogmanay,' we called.

'And mony happy ones tae yis,' called back the New Year dragon in six different voices, before weaving away into the dark; and the village came to us, milky blue and window-glowing under the moon.

The doors were open, there was no need to knock. 'Come in! Come in! And a happy New Year. Set yisselves down and have a droppie. My, but the wee'ns are frozen. Ye'll have ginger wine and a bit of shortbread, bairnies, will ye no? That's right, Calum. Help yisself, laddie.'

So we went on from Dollopy Kirst's to the Renwicks, to the Sturrocks, to Teeny-face-Troon and Conn Barnet's, to the canny, who poured out fingers of sherry in the hope that the bottle would do again next year, and to the lavish, who tilted tumblerfuls into our bright-eyed grandmother; and all had a drink from our bottle and we all had a pull at theirs.

We went to all the houses we knew till the light of the first day came and we were muddled and fuddled and mumbling happy nonsense to each other, full of cake and goodwill after the loving night.

For the spirit of Hogmanay was real and tangible. It wasn't just a great overstuffing. It was the smiles on faces normally stern and the friendliness in eyes often hostile. it was the reminder that people are good. It was the hour when everything you wanted seemed suddenly to be within reach; the spell of the promise of a new start, a New Year in which wishes could come true and dreams be caught, when our secret, ideal selves could become flesh-

and-blood real, if we kept our resolutions. It was that no one ever said, 'Thank God that's over.' It was Crabbie's Green Ginger Wine and shortbread.

from *Wild Honey Time*
M. O'Donoghue

Auld Lang Syne

Should auld acquaintance be forgot,
  And never brought to mind?
Should auld acquaintance be forgot,
  And auld lang syne!

CHORUS
For auld lang syne, my dear,
  For auld lang syne,
We'll tak a cup o' kindness yet
  For auld lang syne.

And surely ye'll be your pint stowp!
  And surely I'll be mine!
And we'll tak a cup o' kindness yet,
  For auld lang syne.

We twa hae run about the braes,
  And pou'd the gowans fine:
But we've wander'd mony a weary fitt,
  Sin' auld lang syne.

We twa hae paidl'd in the burn
  Frae morning sun till dine:
But seas between us braid hae roar'd
  Sin' auld lang syne.

And there's a hand, my trusty fiere!
  And gie's a hand o' thine!
And we'll tak a right gude-willie waught
  For auld lang syne.

Robert Burns

New Year Customs and Folklore

The turn of the year has always been regarded as very special, a time for omens, presents and superstitions, and for traditions based on 'start as you mean to go on.'

The 'cream, crop or flower of the well' custom was widespread throughout Britain and noted in Herefordshire, Monmouthshire and Northumberland. There was a rush to draw the first water of the new year, as it was said to have exceptional supernatural properties and be very lucky. In parts of Scotland, all the dairy utensils were washed with part of the cream of the well, and the cows given the rest to drink.

Here we bring new water
From the well so clear.
For to worship God with,
This happy New Year . . .

Superstitions

In Yorkshire it was considered unlucky to come into a house with empty hands on New Year's morning, while in Lincolnshire, boys used to present small pieces of wood at doors, or be led in and out of the house by the wood. At Willoughton the cry was 'Here's a little bit o' wood, And I hope it'll do you good!' The wood then had to be burnt at once.

It was considered very unlucky to take a light out of the house on New Year's Day, and in fact nothing should be carried out of the house, but as much as possible brought in. It was even known for dust to be swept in and for doorsteps to be sanded so that bits would stick to visitors shoes. In Sussex it was considered lucky to bring mud into the house in January; this mud was called 'January butter'.

In Worcestershire and Gloucestershire it was thought very unlucky to do any washing on New Year's Day, as it's a death omen – 'lest you wash a child away', and also in Devon where the saying goes – 'lest you wash a friend away'.

New Year Cakes

In Suffolk they ate special lucky triangular cakes and drank elderberry wine before midnight. Coventry 'God-cakes', also triangular and filled with a kind of mincemeat, were sent as presents. In St Alban's, Herts special buns, called 'pope ladies' were eaten early in the morning of New Year's Day. They were long and narrow, shaped like a female figure, and had two currants for eyes. Until the 1860s boys used to sell cakes early in the morning in the Cambridge area. They were rather like hot cross buns without the cross.

In Northumberland they ate 'fadge' or rich cake to symbolize brotherly concord and union and in the Highlands of Scotland, New Year's Day was known as the 'Day of Little Christmas'. The head of the house gave a dram of whisky to every member of the household, followed by a breakfast of half-boiled sowen cakes to bring good luck.

New Year Gifts

Apple 'Gifting' was very common at one time with decorated apples given as a sign of friendship, good health and good luck in the year to come. The 'gift' was an apple smeared with flour or meal which was then stuck with oats, grains of wheat, corn or raisins. Three sticks were pushed into it to make a stand, and a skewer pushed into one side as a handle. The top was decorated with sprigs of sweet smelling evergreen, like box, yew, or thyme, and this in turn was hung with hazelnuts. Finally the 'gift' was dusted with wheat flour and some parts were touched up with gold leaf. The apple was a symbol of sweetness, the box or yew of fertility, and the nuts of immortality. In South Wales the apple gifts are known as the Calennig and children take them round from early morning till noon. At Ripon, Yorkshire, it was on Christmas Day that choirboys brought baskets of red apples, each decorated with a sprig of rosemary, and gave them to members of the congregation in return for money. In the cider country of Herefordshire, apple gifts also were known and taken from door to door, but at Castlemorton and Longdon in Worcestershire until the 1950s, children visited farmhouses on New Year's morning and sang this song without taking a breath!

Bud well, bear well, God send you fare well;
Every sprig and every spray
A bushel of apples next New Year's day.
A happy New Year
A pocket full of money
A cellar full of beer.
Please give me a New Year's gift.

At Hastings in Sussex, tradesmen threw out their surplus stock of Christmas apples, and these were scrambled for by fishermen and boys who went to the shops and shouted, 'Throw out! turn out' and at Driffield in Yorkshire boys used to shout to shopkeepers for stock:

Here we are at oor toon end
A shoulder o' mutton and a crown to spend
Hip! Hip! Hooray! and scramble for pennies.

OTHER NEW YEAR GIFTS

At one time gloves were customary gifts, very often to secure favour, and where money was given instead this was called 'glove money'. In the sixteenth century when pins were first invented, they were given as presents to ladies, and gave rise to the expression 'pin-money'.

OTHER NEW YEAR CRIES

This cry was common in Shropshire, Hereford-shire and Gloucestershire:

I wish you a Merry Christmas, and a Happy New Year,
A pocket full of money and a cellar full of beer,
A good fat pig to last you all the year.
Please to give me a New Year's Gift!

and also:

God bless the master of this house
And the good missis too,
And all the little children
That about the table go.
I wish you a Merry Christmas
and a Happy New Year,
And a good fat pig in the larder
to last you all the year.

Out of Scotland, New Year parties are tradition-ally more restrained. In Lincolnshire, Geoffrey Robinson remembers his grandmother's party and an amazingly eccentric musician:

When the time came for Charlie Clay to perform at the New Year's party, all the guests squeezed into the living-room, some moving from the sitting-room, others from the kitchen, where they had congregated in small groups to play chess, or to play cards, or to talk. Charlie sat down at the piano waiting for everyone to settle into silence. He was small and thin, except that between the wings of his open fustian jacket there was an enormous expanse of check waistcoat. It was remarkable that anyone so spare in face, arms and legs, could have so huge a paunch. Across the acres of waistcoat was a heavy gold watch-chain hung profusely with bundles of seals and gold medallions. He was entirely bald, apart from tufts of light brown hair over his ears and extending backwards round the lower part of his head, but the high pink dome of his skull was complemented by a pointed imperial beard, in the fashion of the Prince of Wales. Between these two extremities was a pale oval face dominated by a pair of large gold-rimmed spectacles. Charlie Clay was so short-sighted that the thick lenses showed concentric circles diminishing in diameter and receding, apparently, into the very back of his head where, as if at the end of a tunnel, twinkled two distant eyes, intensely blue, but reduced in size by the lenses to those of a fieldmouse.

All preparations completed and the audience assem-bled, Charlie moved the stool as close to the piano as his stomach allowed and had a preliminary canter over the keyboard by way of a series of brilliant runs, arpeggios, trills and appoggiaturas, all improvised and played with tremendous panache, cascading from one end of the keyboard to the other. Eventually the torrent of notes began to settle into one definite key, and Charlie leaned back on the piano stool, lifted his eyes to the ceiling, opened his mouth, and began to sing in a light tenor. Most of his songs were about the perils of matrimony, but strain my memory as I will, I can remember the names of only three of them – 'My Wife's Relations', 'Leeds Owd Church' and 'The Black Pudding'. Charlie's repertoire was in fact very large, but he was never at a loss for the music because he played by ear. Somtimes, however, he needed to be reminded of the words, so he carried in his pocket a few grubby pieces of paper to which he referred at intervals. As he warmed to his themes, Charlie's eyes darted about amongst the audience in delight. He rolled in mirth around the circumference of the piano stool, his beard wagging and his arms performing the most extraordinary arabesques. For him there was no thumping of a few stale chords as an accompaniment. Every song had its own particular setting – mocking trills, thuds of derision, menacing runs down to the lower registers when disaster impended, light-hearted runs upwards when all was well again, and always air, buoyancy and bravura in the playing. Yet the piano never drowned the clarity of the words. The tempo varied constantly. At very dramatic moments in the recitals Charlie stopped playing altogether, only to resume with long intricate cadenzas to hold everyone on edge waiting for the happy dénouement when the theme galloped joyfully away again. Year after year the same songs were repeated, and year after year the family were falling about helpless with merriment – with two exceptions. Aunt Kate pretended to be a little amused, and Charlie's wife, the former Miss Utting, sat silent, impassive and disapproving.

from *Hedingham Harvest*
GEOFFREY ROBINSON

WASSAILING THE APPLE ORCHARDS

Traditionally this took place between Christmas and the 18 Jan – Old Twelfth Night. It is undergoing a revival at Much Marcle in Herefordshire, Norton Fitzwarren in Somerset, North Devon, and in the Bristol area, and the custom has continued at the Butchers Arms, Carhampton, in Somerset on Old Twelfth Night.

The aim is to protect the trees from evil spirits and to ensure a plentiful crop of apples in the next season. The oldest or best tree in the orchard is chosen to represent them all. This is known as the Apple Tree Man and fêted as the guardian of the orchard. Cider is poured on the roots, and pieces of toast or cake soaked in cider are either laid in its fork or hung from the branches for the robins, who were considered as the guardian spirits of the trees. Sometimes the tips of the branches are dipped into cider. The tree was then toasted with cider and songs. Then trees were rapped and sometimes their bark was torn in order to help dislodge insects. A huge din was made to drive away the evil spirits and wake the sleeping trees. Originally trays and buckets were beaten and cow horns blown, but more recently shot-guns are fired through the topmost branches.

Throughout the country the ceremonies and songs differ slightly from place to place. In South Devon they encircle the trees and drink this toast three times:

Here's to thee, old apple tree,
Whence thou may'st bud, and whence thou may'st blow!
And whence thou may'st bear apples enow!
Hatsfull! Capsfull! Bushel-bushel-sacksfull,
And my pockets full too! Huzza!

In Sussex, the custom was known as 'Worsling' when on New Year's Day, boys visited the orchards, encircled the trees and chanted:

Stand fast, bear well top,
Pray God send us a howling crop;
Every twig, apples big;
Every bough, apples enow,
Hats full, caps full,
Full quarter sacks full.

This was followed by a great shout and rapping the trees with sticks. At Anstead Brook near Haslemere in Surrey, the ceremony took place on

New Year's Eve and survived until the mid-nineteenth century. It was also known as 'Howling' or 'Youling' and widespread in western and southern counties and parts of Wales. After the tree ceremony, the Howlers processed to the farmer's house or local pub where having sung for admission, they were fêted with ale.

'WASSAILING THE WINTER ORCHARDS'

The sun shining on particular days was always, time out of mind, a favourite rural notion as regards good luck, and it is still a prevalent idea that if the sun shines through the apple trees of the orchards on Christmas Day, there will be an abundant crop of apples the following year.

The chief observance connected with apple orchards was that of wassailing the trees, the term derived from the Saxon *waes hael* (water of health), and thus the wassail or health-bowl became a popular institution.

This wassailing the fruit trees is a custom derived from very old times, and was observed by farmers of the last century. I have met with persons who have been at its celebration in rural districts, and I have received reliable information of its observance last Christmas.

The following account has been given me of the wassailing as witnessed some years since at a farm on the banks of the Teme in this county. The eve of the Twelfth Day, or Old Christmas Eve, was the time observed for this rural festivity, which was originally intended to secure a blessing to the fruits of the earth, but at last the superstitious idea was taken up, that if the wassailing was omitted, the produce of the orchards would be very little. This injunction was, therefore, generally borne in mind, repeated, and acted upon:

> *Wassail the trees that they may bear*
> *You many an apple and many a pear;*
> *Or more or less fruit they will bring*
> *As you do give them wassailing.*

Therefore, on the evening mentioned, the farmer with his neighbours being assembled, they proceeded to an elevated wheat field, where twelve small fires were lighted, and a large one in the centre, these fires being generally considered as representative of our Saviour and the twelve apostles, though in some places they bear the vulgar appellation of Old Meg and her daughters.

Jugs of prime old cider having been brought, healths are joyously drunk with abundant hurrahing from a circle formed round the central fire. The party afterwards adjourn to an orchard, and there encircling one of the best bearing trees, and not forgetting cider, sprinkle the tree, while one of the party carols forth the following verse:

> *Here's to thee, old apple tree,*
> *Whence thou may'st bud, and whence thou may'st blow,*
> *And whence thou may'st bear apples enow,*
> *Hats full and caps full,*
> *Bushels full and sacks full,*
> *And my pockets full too.*

A chorus of obstreperous huzzas follows, and the whole party then returns to the farmhouse, where a bountiful supper with libations of cider, the result of former wassailing, awaits them.

That this observance is not yet given up in some secluded places is evident from what I have heard of an old farmer, who stated to a visitor that his neglect of wassailing one year caused the failure of his crop of apples!

Pear trees, of course, take the benefit of the wassailing process jointly with the apple, so that except historically there are but few things to be gathered referable to the pear alone. A variety may, however, be mentioned, called 'the bloody pear' from its sanguine coloured pulp when cut into, and I was once told that an orchard on the ground where the Battle of Evesham was fought, would only produce this 'bloody pear'!

> *Come, let us hye and quaff a cheery bowl,*
> *Let cider now wash sorrow from the soul!*

WASSAIL!

Trad arr. J. Coppin/P. Beer/P. Burgess ©

Key D

1. Fine joll-y hood-en-ing boys Late-ly come from town For

app-les or for mon-ey we search the coun-try round.

What you please to give us happ-y we shall be

God bless ev'-ry poor man who's got an app-le tree. *Hats-ful, caps-ful,*

CHORUS

half a bush-el bag-ful, God bless ev'-ry poor man who's

rall
got an app-le tree. 2. There was an old man who had an old cow How to

keep the cow warm He did-n't know how. He built up a barn for to

keep the cow warm And a cup of good ci-der will do him no harm.

CHORUS

Do him no harm. Do him no harm, And a cup of good ci-der will

do him no harm.

3. The girt dog of Langport he burnt his long tail
    and this is the night we go singing wassail
    O master and missus now we must be gone
    God bless all this house till we do come again.

    CH: *Do come again, do come again,*
    God bless all this house till we do come again.

4. Here's to the master a ten gallon man
    who always gets tiddly whenever he can
    And here's to the mistress when master's not in
    who goes to the cupboard and brings out the gin.

    CH: *Brings out the gin, brings out the gin,*
    who goes to the cupboard and brings out the gin.

6. Here comes a ship out in full sail
   ploughs the wide ocean in many a gale

   CH: *For singing wassail, wassail, wassail,*
   and joy come to our jolly wassail.

7. Come knock at the knocker and ring at the bell
   I know you'll reward us for singing so well.

   CH: *For singing wassail, wassail, wassail,*
   and jolly come to our jolly wassail.

A Saxon word for 'good health!' gives its name to the wassaillers who toured the neighbourhood with their wassail bowl. To ensure plenty of carol-singing, the wassail bowl would be topped up at each stop with punch, usually consisting of a mixture similar to hot cider, gin, nutmeg, and sugar. As one of the verses implies, the houses which provided a good helping of gin were among the most popular! This medley of wassails moves from east to west. It begins with a Kent 'hoodening' song followed by a wassail song known in Devon, Somerset, and Dorset. Next there's a tune written by Paul and Phil, and the medley ends with our version of the Bodmin Wassail.

If such a panacea for the cares and sorrows of life can be accepted, the cider-cup must be considered deserving of general approval, and in thus offering it, I trust the orchards may have an abundant crop of fruit.

from *Worcestershire Naturalists' Club* records (1847–1896)

OTHER NEW YEAR CUSTOMS

Burning the Bush was widespread in Worcestershire and the West Midlands, and lingered on in the Malvern area until the early 1900s. 'Globes' of hawthorn were plaited by farmwomen as a fire and fertility charm. They were then baked in the oven and hung up in the kitchen until the following year. While the women worked, the men went 'burning the bush' by firing the old globe in the field, and ran with it over thirteen ridges, and allowing the falling ashes to fertilise the fields and bring a good crop.

'Stanging' was a custom in Cumberland and Westmorland where men carrying poles and baskets seized people and demanded money. Any man who refused would be mounted on a pole or 'stang' and any woman put in a basket (there is a 'Riding the Stang' bas-relief in Montacute House, Somerset)

At Kirkwall on Orkney street football lasted up to 6 hours, as large teams tried to take a 3lb ball back to opposite ends of the town, and at Hubberholme in the Yorkshire Dales, a 'candle-auction' was held to decide the letting of some land.

New Year Divinations

The first new moon of the year was consulted for love and marriage prospects: In Yorkshire and Lincolnshire, a girl had to look at the new moon through a silk handkerchief, and 'she will see as many moons as years that will elapse before she marries'.

Weather and Plant Lore: St Faine's Day

Whether the weather be snow or rain
We are sure to see the flower of St Faine.
Rain come but seldom and often snow
And yet the Vibernum is sure to blow.

from Buckinghamshire:

If the Calends of January be smiling and gay,
You'll have wintry weather till the Calends of May.

From Devon:

If New Year's Day happen on a Saturday, the winter
will be mean, the summer hot, and the harvest late.

THE LAST DAYS OF CHRISTMAS

'But we still burn the holly,
On Twelfth Night: burn the holly
As people do: the holly,
Ivy, and mistletoe.'

Thomas Hardy

THE FIRST WEEK OF JANUARY

Just after New Year is often a time of harsh weather, and the difficulties this brings to farming and country life can never be underestimated. In this extract from *Lorna Doone*, R.D. Blackmore gives a vivid picture of one man's struggle to protect his livelihood on the hills of Exmoor:

It must have snowed most wonderfully to have made that depth of covering in about eight hours. For one of Master Stickles' men, who had been out all night, said that no snow had begun to fall until nearly midnight. And here it was blocking up the doors, stopping the ways, and the water-courses, and making it very much worse to walk than in a saw-pit newly used. However, we trudged along in a line; I first, and the other men after me; trying to keep my track, but finding legs and strength not up to it. Most of all, John Fry was groaning; certain that his time was come, and sending messages to his wife, and blessings to his children. For all this time it was snowing harder than it had ever snowed before, so far as a man might guess at it; and the leaden depth of sky came down, like a mine turned upside down on us. Not that the flakes were so very large; for I have seen much larger flakes in a shower in March, while sowing peas; but there was no room between them, neither any relaxing, nor any change of direction.

Watch, like a good and faithful dog, followed us very cheerfully, leaping out of the depth which took him over his back and ears already, even in the level places; while in the drifts he might have sunk to any distance out of sight and never found his way up again. However, we helped him now and then, especially through the gaps and gateways; and so after a deal of floundering, some laughter and a little swearing, we came safe to the lower meadow, where most of our flock were hurdled.

But behold, there was no flock at all! None, I mean, to be seen anywhere; only at one corner of the field, by the eastern end, where the snow drove in, a great white billow, as high as a barn and as broad as a house. This great drift was rolling and curling beneath the violent blast, tufting and coming with rustling swirls, and carved (as in patterns of cornice) where the grooving chisel of the wind swept round. Ever and again, the tempest snatched little whiffs from the channelled edges, twirled them round, and made them dance over the chine of the monster pile, then let them lie like herring-bones, or the seams of sand where the tide had been. And all the while from the smothering sky, more and more fiercely at every blast, came the pelting pitiless arrows, winged with murky white, and pointed with barbs of frost.

But although, for people who had no sheep, the sight was a very fine one (so far at least as the weather permitted any sight at all); yet for us, with our flock beneath it, this great mount had but little charm. Watch began to scratch at once, and to howl along the sides of it; he knew that his charge was buried there, and his business taken from him. But we four men set to in earnest, digging with all our might and main, shovelling away at the great white pile, and fetching it into the meadow. Each man made for himself a cave, scooping at the soft cold flux, which slid upon him at every stroke, and throwing it out behind him, in piles of castled fancy. At last we drove our tunnels in (for we worked indeed for the lives of us), and all converging towards the middle, held our tools and listened.

The other men heard nothing at all; or declared that they heard nothing, being anxious now to abandon the matter, because of the chill in their feet and knees. But I said, 'Go, if you choose, all of you. I will work it out by myself, you pie-crusts': and upon that they gripped their shovels, being more or less Englishmen; and the least drop of English blood is worth the best of any other, when it comes to lasting out.

But before we began again, I laid my head well into the chamber; and there I heard a faint 'ma-a-ah', coming through some ells of snow, like a plaintive buried hope, or a last appeal. I shouted aloud to cheer him up, for I knew what sheep it was, to wit the most valiant of all the wethers, who had met me when I came home from London, and had been so glad to see me. And then we all fell to again; and very soon we hauled him out. Watch took charge of him at once, with an air of noblest patronage, lying on his frozen fleece, and licking him all over his face and feet, to restore his warmth to him. Then fighting Tom jumped up at once, and made a little butt at Watch, as if nothing had ever ailed him, and then set off to a shallow place, and looked for something to nibble at.

Further in, and close under the bank, where they had huddled themselves for warmth, we found all the rest of the poor sheep packed as closely as if they were in a great pie. It was strange to observe how their vapour, and breath, the moisture exuding from their wool, had scooped, as it were, a covered room for them, lined with a ribbing of deep yellow snow. Also the churned snow beneath their feet was as yellow as gamboge. Two or three of the weaklier hoggets were dead, from want of air, and from pressure; but more than three score were as lively as ever: though cramped and stiff for a little while.

'However shall we get them home?' John Fry asked in great dismay, when we had cleared about a dozen of them; which we were forced to do very carefully, so as not to fetch the roof down. 'No manner of manning to draive 'un, drough all they giry driftnesses.'

'You see to this place, John,' I replied, as we leaned on our shovels a moment, and the sheep came rubbing around us: 'Let no more of them out for the present; they are better where they be. Watch, here boy, keep them!'

Watch came, and with his little scut of a tail cocked as sharp a duty; and I set him at the narrow mouth of the great snow antre. All the sheep siddled away, and got closer, that the other sheep might be bitten first, as the foolish things imagine; whereas no good sheep-dog even so much as lips a sheep to turn it.

Then of the outer sheep (all now snowed and frizzled like a lawyer's wig) I took the two finest and heaviest; and with one beneath my right arm, and the other beneath my left, I went straight home to the upper sheppey, set them inside and fastened them. Sixty-and-six I took home in that way, two at a time on each journey; and the work grew harder and harder each time, as the drifts of snow were deepening. No man should meddle with them: I was resolved to try my strength against the strength of the elements; and try I did, ay and proved it. A certain fierce

delight burned in me, as the struggle grew harder; but rather would I die than yield; and at last I finished it. People talk of it to this day; but none can tell what the labour was, who had not felt that snow and wind.

from *Lorna Doone*
R. D. BLACKMORE

TOFFEE JOINS

In the north of England, 'toffee joins' were arranged in the long winter evenings. Neighbours met in houses to play cards, gossip, and flirt while a mixture of butter and treacle was stirred in a brass pan over the fire. When the toffee was ready it was shared out and eaten.

At Muker in Yorkshire, just after New Year, there was the unusual festival of 'Muker Awd Roy'. This four day celebration began on the Wednesday before Old Christmas Day (6 January) and continued until the weekend. It was based at the three village inns and food that had been collected the night before was made freely available to all-comers. There were market-stalls, and several villagers marched round the houses to the beat of a drum singing:

> *Now T'awd Roy is come,*
> *Let us beat up the drum,*
> *And call all our neighbours together.*
> *And when they appear*
> *Let us make them such cheer,*
> *As will keep out the wind and the weather.*

On Thursday and Friday there were outdoor sports such as hurdle-jumping, trotting matches and shooting competitions; work was suspended, the inns were open day and night, and local fiddlers and wandering musicians kept everyone entertained.

The grand finale on the Saturday night was the *Princum Prancum*, a cushion or 'whishing' dance held at the Queen's Head.

Muker Awd Roy was probably a survival of an ancient feast of Epiphany – with the term 'Awd Roy' having the same origins as '*Le jour des Rois*' – the day of the Kings.

5 JANUARY (OLD CHRISTMAS EVE)
EPIPHANY EVE

This is still believed by some to be the actual Christmas Eve with all the customs and superstitions associated with it – at midnight cows go down on their knees, bees hum in their hives, and Holy Thorns blossom. Pilgrimages were made as late as early 1900s to one of the Holy Thorns.

LEGENDS OF THE HOLY THORN

The Glastonbury Thorn is the most famous and involves the story of Joseph of Arimathea, a wealthy merchant, who frequently visited the West Country. In 63 AD he headed a mission to Somerset, but met with hostility and disbelief wherever he went. Not to be beaten he prayed for a sign or miracle and then one day, while climbing Wearyall Hill near Glastonbury, his prayers were answered. Taking a moment's rest, he fixed his pilgrim's staff in the ground, and it immediately blossomed into a thorn tree. This supernatural miracle made all the Somerset people who came to see the wonder very attentive to Joseph's preaching of the Gospel. And so the legend was born. It is said to blossom twice a year – at Christmas and Easter. It is a variety from Palestine – *Crataegus monogyna biflora* – and has a cluster of small white flowers flecked with pink. The tradition of sending sprigs of the Thorn to the Royal Family began before the Reformation and still continues.

There are many others said to flower at Christmas – at Clooneaven House at Lynmouth in Devon, at Stoneyhurst in Lancashire, at Quainton in Bucks, and one was seen in Middlesex in 1672 by Elias Ashmole 'with green leaves, faire buds, and full flowers, all thick and very beautiful.' At West Buckland, Somerset – where at midnight on 5 January 'Old Christmas' – legend has it that the flowers blossom for ten minutes before returning to buds until ready to flower again in the Spring. At Hill Pill, in Gloucestershire on the Forest of Dean side of the River Severn, a holy thorn served as a mark for Severn navigators.

There are several in Herefordshire. The Holy Thorn at Orcop was still visited by many people

'THE FLOWERING OF THE THORN'

Music: J. Coppin/J. Broomhall ©

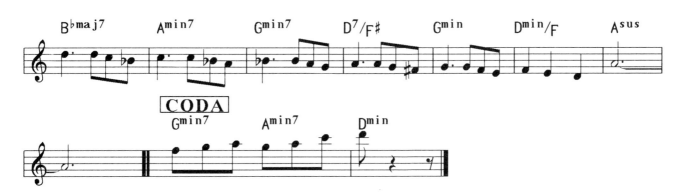

ORDER: A × 4/B × 1/A × 2/C × 1/B × 1/A × 4/D × 1/B × 2/C × 1/A × 4

This tune is inspired by a Leonard Clark poem of the same name, and the Legend of the Holy Thorn.

on 5 January in the last 1960s. At Eaton Bishop, Herefordshire in the churchyard of St Michael & All Angels, there was a Holy Thorn bush which had been brought back from Jerusalem in 1904 by the then Rector Rev. Charles Burrough. This bush has now died, but has been replaced with another Holy Thorn from Kew Gardens which was planted in 1990 in memory of the artist, Derek Mobbs, by his family.

The power of the Holy Thorns is not to be underestimated – there's an old saying 'never pick Holy Thorn on Old Christmas Eve when you hear the cracking of the buds, or you will receive a curse.' In Herefordshire, a man at Clehonger, Herefordshire who tried to cut down the Holy Thorn in his garden, gave up after blood flowed from the trunk after the first blow of the axe. And a farmer who suffered a broken arm, a broken leg, and his farmhouse burnt down after cutting down the Holy Thorn at Acton Beauchamp. A Holy Thorn, rumoured to have grown from a cutting of the Glastonbury Thorn itself, made a brief appearance in a garden at Sutton Poyntz, Dorset in 1844. 150 people came to see it blossom on Old Christmas Eve, but violent scenes took place, fences were broken and the plant became so damaged that it died.

The Rev. Francis Kilvert writes of visiting a Holy Thorn in Herefordshire:

BREDWARDINE VICARAGE, HEREFORDSHIRE
Monday, 7 January, 1878.
I went to the little farmhouse of Dolfach on the hill to see the Holy Thorn there in blossom. The tree (a graft from the old Holy Thorn at Tibberton now cut down) bloomed on Old Christmas Eve and there were 15 people watching round the tree to see it blow at midnight. I found old John Parry sitting at tea by the cheerful firelight in the chimney corner. His kind daughter gave me a bit of a spray of the Holy Thorn which was gathered from the tree at midnight, old Christmas Eve. She set great store by the spray and always gathered and kept a bit each year. The blossoms were not fully out and the leaves were scarcely unfolded but the daughter of the house assured me that the little white bud clusters would soon come out into full blow if put in soft water. The parent tree is a hawthorn and blossoms again in May. It was the first bit of Holy Thorn I had ever seen.

from *Kilvert's Diary*
REV. FRANCIS KILVERT

6 JANUARY (OLD CHRISTMAS DAY) EPIPHANY OR TWELFTH DAY

As one of the oldest Christian festivals, Epiphany celebrates the Adoration of the Magi – the Three Kings. Their arrival at the stable was celebrated by a Twelfth Night party, and in many parts of the world is a public holiday. Many of the Epiphany customs have moved back to New Year or Christmas and the belief in 6 January as the actual Christmas Day (on the old pre-1752 calendar) was widespread. In the 1850s, Davies Gilbert tell us of an old couple in Herefordshire who used to walk to church in full dress, and after trying in vain to enter, walked back and read the service at home.

In Ireland, the day is called Women's Christmas. Candles are lit for the last time, there is a Thanksgiving drink after the meal, and it is believed that all water becomes wine between sunset on 5 January and sunrise on 6 January.

Twelfth Day was a special holiday for horses: many country people believed that anyone who rode or drove a horse was certain to meet with an accident, and also that if they were rested it prevented them being difficult all year.

TWELFTH NIGHT REVELS

The last night of Christmas was celebrated with large scale parties and feasting, the centrepeice of which was the Twelfth Cake, a tradition that goes back as far as the mediaeval court of Edward II. The cutting of the cake determined the election of the King and Queen of Twelfth Night. A bean and a pea were inserted in the cake before baking, and he who had a slice with the bean became King, and she who had a piece with the pea was elected Queen. The King and Queen could then order games and forfeits just like the old Lord of Misrule and the King of the Saturnalian revels.

Now, now the mirth comes
With the cake full of plums,
Where Beane's the King of the sport here;
Beside we must know,
The Pea also
Must revell, as Queene, in the court here . . .

from ROBERT HERRICK'S 'Twelfe Night'

The Twelfth Cake or *Gâteau des Rois* is still popular in France, and a high point of the season. It is the origin of describing someone who has good luck as *Il a trouve la fève au gâteau* (he has found a bean in his cake).

In 1830 an interesting variation took place in Cornwall, when the farmers of Sennen held a Twelfth Night feast, and one of the dishes was a 'four-and-twenty-blackbird pie'. Revels of another kind still occur at Haxey, near Scunthorpe, where The Hood Game is still played with two teams competing with a two-foot leather cylinder 'football' or 'hood.'

Wassailing the apple trees continues in many other areas, but in Worcestershire, Herefordshire and Gloucestershire the 6 January is the time for Twelfth Night Fires, ancient magic for fertility and as insurance against a poor harvest. Twelve fires were lit and hopefully the flames leapt and danced in simulation of future fields of waving grain. One fire dedicated to Judas Iscariot was immediately stamped out and the ashes scattered, while round a thirteenth and larger fire representing Christ, sat the farmer with his family, servants and friends eating plumcake and toasting the next harvest in warm cider. Then the party went to the cowshed carrying a special cake with a hole in it. The best cow or ox was led in. There followed a toast:

Fill your cups, my merry men all!
For here's the best ox in the stall,
Oh! He is the best ox, of that there's no mistake
And so let us crown him with the Twelfth cake

and the cake was placed upon one of his horns, and encouraged to toss his head and throw the cake into the air. If it fell before him, it belonged to the bailiff, if behind to the mistress.

A slight variation was to stick a large cake on a cow's horns, and all drink to the health of the cow: 'Here's to thee –, and to thy white horn, Pray God send us a good crop of corn . . . ' If the cake fell in front of the cow it belonged to the cowman, if it fell behind to the dairymaid.

In Ireland, a variation of the Twelfth Night Fires was to set up twelve candles and one large one round a sieve full of oats – to represent Christ and his disciples as the lights of the world. In Staffordshire there were Twelfth Day fires and they called the 6 January 'Blaze Night'. On Holly Night at Brough in Westmorland, torches were tied to branches of the Holling or Holly tree, procured by the landlords of the two leading inns of the town. This was then carried in procession by Joseph Ling, the local strongman, led by the band and accompanied by cheering spectators also carrying torches. Finally the nearly burnt-out tree was fought for by supporters of the two inns, with the successful pub then providing a 'merry neet' paid for by the losing side. This custom commemorated the Star of Bethlehem on Old Christmas Eve, and resembles a similar ceremony performed in Normandy where the builders of Brough Castle originated.

SAYINGS AND SUPERSTITIONS

It was believed that if Old Christmas Day came during a waxing moon, a good year would follow, and if during a waning moon, a hard year. If the sun shine through the apple trees on that day it will be a good cider year. A popular saying from Devon was, Child born upon Old Christmas Day is good, and wise, and fair, and gay.

Twelfth Night marks the end of the Christmas season and all decorations must be taken down from houses by then, or bad luck will follow. In churches all evergreens must be removed by Candlemas Eve (1 February). Some people even sent servants to sweep private pews in case a stray leaf had been overlooked. All evergreens must be burnt out of doors, and this tradition has been carried to the USA, where household decorations are burnt in parks.

An old saying from Cheshire runs: 'Burn all the Christmas decorations in the shape of holly and ivy by Old Christmas Day, or your house will be haunted by evil spirits all the year'.

TWELFTH NIGHT

Our candles, lit, re-lit, have gone down now:
There were the dry twigs tipped with buds of fire,
But red and white have twisted into air,
The little shadow stills its to and fro.

We draw familiar faces from the wall
But all is part of a dismantling dark
Which works upon the heart that must not break,
Upon the carried thing that must not fall.

Needles are shivered from the golden bough,
Our leaves and paper nothings are decayed
And all amazements of the Phoenix breed
Are cupboarded in dust, dull row on row.

While branchwork set upon a whitened ground
Climbs out into a vortex of wild flame.
The substance of this deep Midwinter dream:
A scale of ash upon a frozen wind.

Our candles, lit, re-lit, have gone down now:
Only the tears, the veils, the hanging tree
Whose burning gauze thins out across the sky,
Whose brightness dies to image. And the snow.

PETER SCUPHAM

7 JANUARY ST DISTAFF'S DAY

Traditionally this is the day when women began to spin and go back to work after the holiday.

Partly work and partly play
You must on St Distaff's Day:
From the plough soon free your team;
Then come home and fother them:
If the maids a-spinning go,
Burn the flax and fire the tow.
Bring in pails of water then,
Let the maids bewash the men.
Give St Distaff all the right:
Then bid Christmas sport good night,
And next morrow every one
To his own vocation

ROBERT HERRICK

There's an old Well Custom on St Agnes in the Scilly Isles. St Warna's Well is cleaned out, and there are mystic ceremonies followed by feasting. St Warna was believed to send them shipwrecks and control the island's fortune.

PLOUGH SUNDAY –
FIRST SUNDAY AFTER EPIPHANY

The plough was blessed in church, and before work was resumed the next day.

PLOUGH MONDAY

This was a day of great festivity centred on the Fool Plough Procession. Throughout much of England there were Plough boys, stots, jags or witchers who went round disguised like mummers to collect money for a feast. In Lincolnshire at Revesby the Plough Monday play resembles a mummer's play, with the Fool being killed during a sword dance, but rises again with the words: ' . . . I am not slain: But I will rise, your sport for to advance, And with you all, brave boys, I'll have a dance.'

In the 1830s an anchor was dragged through the streets of Hartlepool on Twelfth Day rather in the manner of the Fool Plough tradition, and at Goathland in Yorkshire, the Plough Stots perform a longsword dance descended from the Norsemen over a thousand years ago. In the fenlands of East Anglia until 1914, a man completely covered in straw, the 'Straw Bear', was led round the inns to sing and dance. Now on the Saturday before

Plough Monday there is a Straw Bear Festival at Whittlesey, Cambridgeshire where the Bear dances through the streets collecting for charity.

At Plough Monday ceremonies in Essex, ploughmen used to draw their decorated ploughs round the parishes and threaten to plough up villagers' thresholds unless they gave them money. They would gather in a ring, bend down with their heads together and hum like a bell. At a given signal from the leader, they would fling their heads back so that the resonant hum would suddenly explode into a cry for a donation.

In South Cambridgeshire, Suffolk and Essex there is a tradition of the 'molly dance' and singing by a large team of men and women dancers with blackened faces. They are led by a 'lord' and 'lady' and the team also includes a 'man-woman', – the 'molly'. Plough Monday continues to be celebrated in the villages around Good Easter near Dunmow in Essex.

In this extract from Sybil Marshall's *Fenland Chronicle*, Kate Mary Edwards recalls all the fun she had as a child on Plough Monday:

'Plough Witching'

Living where we did and how we did, we used to make the most of anything a bit out of the ordinary, and we looked for'ard from one special day to the next. Looking back on it now, I'm surprised to see how many high days and holidays there were during the year that we kept, and we certainly made the most of anything children could take part in.

Just after Christmas, there'd be Plough Witching to look for'ard to. This were Plough Monday, and of course I know that this is still kept in churches all over the land. But our Plough Monday ha'n't got nothing to do with churches as I knowed. There were two or three different things about it. For one thing there were the pranks the young fellows got up to, playing tricks on their neighbours. Very often these were real, nasty tricks, and they'd wait until Plough Monday to get their own back on somebody what had done them some injury during the year. Perhaps they'd take a plough in the middle of the night and plough the other fellow's doorway up, or move the water butt so as it stood resting on a bit of its bottom rim, a-leaning up outside the door. Then when the man o' the house opened the door afore it were light next morning, the tub 'ould fall in and the water slosh all over the floor o' the house-place, for the poor woman to clean up on her hands and knees afore the children could come out o' the bedroom. Very often a gang of young men 'ould go round the Fen taking gates off their hinges and throwing 'em in the nearest dyke, so that all the horses and cows got out. This sort o' nasty trick gradually died out during my young days, and a good thing too I reckon.

Then there were the Straw Bear and the Molly Dancers. The Molly Dancers 'ould come round the Fen from Ramsey and Walton all dressed up. One would have a fiddle, and another a dulcimer, or perhaps a concertina and play while the rest danced. This were really special for Christmas Eve, but o' course the dancers couldn't be everywhere at once on one day, so they used to go about on any other special day to make up for it.

They'd go from pub to pub, and when they'd finished there, they'd go to any houses or cottages where they stood a chance o' getting anything. If we ha'n't got any money to give them, at least they never went away without getting a hot drink. Sometimes it 'ould be hot beer. In pubs they used to hot the beer by sticking a cone-shaped metal container down into the glowing turf fire, with the beer in it. Then it would be made syruppy sweet with brown sugar, and spiced with ginger, served with a long rod o' glass to break the sugar up and stir it with, for 2d a pint. At home it might be done in the same way, or it might simply have a red hot poker plunged into it. Sometimes the Molly Dancers got home-made elderberry wine, well-sugared and made scalding hot and spiced with cloves. A lot of the Fen women were very good at making wine, and their elderberry would be so dark and rich as you could hardly tell it from port wine.

So a good tumbler full of that, all sweet and hot and spicy, were worth dancing for, and kept the cold out till they got to the next cottage.

The Straw Bear were a sort o' ceremony that took place on Plough Monday when I were a child, though my husband says it used to belong to some other day once and only got mixed up with Plough Witching time by chance. A party of men would choose one of their gang to be 'straw bear' and they'd start a-dressing him in the morning ready for their travels round the Fen at night. They saved some o' the straightest, cleanest and shiniest oat straw and bound it all over the man until he seemed to be made of straw from head to foot, with just his face showing. When night came they'd set out from pub to pub and house to house, leading the straw bear on a chain.

When they were asked in, the bear would go down on his hands and knees and caper about and sing and so on. Some parties used to do a play about 'Here I come I, old Beelzebub', and there were another place where one man knocked another one down, and then stood over him and said:

Pains within and pains without
If the devil's in, I'll fetch him out
Rise up and fight again.

I remember hearing about the year when Long Tom were the straw bear. His mates had spent the whole day from early morning getting him 'dorned out, and they were just about ready to start when he were took short and they had to pull all the straw off him quick to let him go to the closet. They weren't half savage with him, I can tell you, and they di'n't let him forget it for a goodish while.

What us children liked best were the Plough Witching, 'cos we could take part in that ourselves. We dressed up in anything we could find and blacked our faces with soot from the chimney to disguise ourselves. Then we went to our neighbours' houses and capered about on their door-ways, or sang a song till they opened the door and let us in. There were a special song as we sung while we shook our collecting tin up and down:

'Ole in yer stocking
'Ole in yer shoe
Please will yer give me a penny or two.
If yew ain't got a penny
A a'penny'll do
An' if yew ain't got an a'penny
Well God bless yew!

Just one! Just one! Just one for the poor old ploughboy!
Just one! Just one! Just one!

This went on right up to the time my own children were little, and for all I know there's still some places where they don't let Plough Monday pass without somebody going a-Plough Witching, but I dessay folks are all too educated and clever to take pleasure in such simple things as that, nowadays.

from *Fenland Chronicle*
SYBIL MARSHALL

JANUARY

The snow has melted now,
Uncovered on the lawn
The holly that we threw
Out when the year was done.
The crimson berries glow
Brilliant against the green,
And on a sculptured bough
Hard, black as ebony,
A robin-redbreast flings
Into the winter sky
His little sparks of song
Like promises of Spring.

DOUGLAS GIBSON

11 JANUARY

The day for Burning the Clavie at Burghead in Grampian, a Midwinter Fire Festival originally held on New Year's Eve before the calendar

Winter

Words: Frank Mansell/Music: J. Coppin ©

1. An op-en gate, a field new ploughed, the
wind north-east u-pon the hill;
A na-ked copse, an
old man bowed, Who walks the road with time to kill;

2. Who climbs the hill as dusk comes down And
thinks of days he used to know,
Whose mind is like a
light-ed town Un-der the lamps of long a-go.

One of Frank Mansell's Cotswold Ballads, *this poem is tinged with deep regret for turning his back on the land, and the struggle of farming in winter.*

change. A burning tar barrel is carried through the streets at night, and people are given pieces from the Clavie for good luck, before it is taken to a small hill near the northern end of the promontory known as the 'Dourie' and left to burn. This custom is also known in Brittany and Russia and is thought to be based upon a worship of Mithras.

13 JANUARY ST HILARY'S DAY

This is supposed to be the coldest day of the year, and a time to wrap up warm and protect susceptible plants from frost. In 1684, 1716, 1740, 1789, and 1814 there were such great freezes that 'Frost Fairs' were held on rivers throughout Britain.

18 JANUARY (OLD TWELFTH NIGHT)

Wassailling the Apple Trees continues at The Butchers Arms, Carhampton in Somerset. (see New Year).

24 JANUARY

St Paul's Day was a public holiday for the miners of Cornwall. It was known as 'Paul Pitcher Day' after the old custom of setting up a water-pitcher and pelting it with stones until it broke. A new one was then brought and carried to the ale-house to be filled with beer. Another favourite custom on 'Paul Pitcher Eve' was to throw broken pitchers against the doors of houses while exclaiming 'St Paul's Eve, and here's a heave!'

1 FEBRUARY CANDLEMAS EVE

At one time Christmas and winter feasting continued right through to this date as this wonderful extract from Fettiplace's Receipt Book describes:

January was always the season for party-going and -giving, at its height from Christmas Day to Twelfth Night but often stretching well beyond that. In the reign of Elizabeth I, Sir William Holles reckoned to begin his Christmas at Allhallowstide and keep it up until Candlemas, November 1 to February 2, three solid months of feasting (when, as his grandson bitterly said, the family fortunes might as well have been poured down the privy). December 25 was a minor feast compared with Twelfth Night, January 6, the chief day of the whole year for entertaining and parties. Country houses up and down the kingdom kept open house with a welcome for allcomers so that, what with friends and relations, guests, servants, villagers and 'strangers', a family like the Fettiplaces at Appleton Manor in Berkshire might expect to feed anything from fifty people upwards twice daily for twelve days on end at Twelfthtide.

Sir William Petre of Ingatestone Hall in Essex sat down to dinner on January 6, 1552 – half a century before Lady Fettiplace's book was written – with over a hundred people, who consumed between them sixteen raised pies, fifteen joints of beef, four of veal, three of pork (including a whole sucking pig), three geese, a brace each of partridge, teal, capons and coneys, a woodcock and one dozen larks, with a whole sheep and much else for supper that night. Entertaining on this scale was quite normal, and remained so until well into the seventeenth century.

from *Eleanor Fettiplace's Receipt Book*
ed. HILARY SPURLING

This is traditionally the day by when all decorations in houses and churches had to be removed or bad luck is bound to follow.

CEREMONY UPON CANDLEMAS EVE

Down with the rosemary, and so
Down with the bays and mistletoe;
Down with the holly, ivy, all
Wherewith ye dressed the Christmas hall;
That so the superstitious find
No one last branch there left behind;
For look, how many leaves there be
Neglected there, maids, trust to me,
So many goblins you shall see.

ROBERT HERRICK

2 FEBRUARY: CANDLEMAS – THE FEAST OF PURIFICATION OF THE VIRGIN, AND THE PRESENTATION OF CHRIST IN THE TEMPLE

Candles are blessed in church, and sometimes snowdrops were put in place of the Christmas evergreens to signify the end of Christmas and the start of Spring. In pagan Rome candles were burned to the goddess Februa, mother of Mars, to drive off evil spirits, so here's another example of the way the early Christian Church substituted a pagan festival.

Down with the rosemary and bays,
Down with the mistletoe:
Instead of holly now upraise
The greener box for show.

The holly hitherto did sway,
Let box now domineer,
Until the dancing Easter day
Or Easter's eve appear . . .

ROBERT HERRICK

Finally some weatherlore from Cumbria:

If Candlemas Day be cloudy an' black,
'Twill carry away aw t'winter on its back;
But it t'sun shine afore it's noon
Winter, depend on't isn't half done.

INFORMATION ON ALBUMS, CAROLS, SONGS AND TUNES:

Song for Loders
Lord of all this Revelling
Gloucestershire Wassail
The Oxen
Wiltshire Carol
Sailor's Carol
The Campden Carol
Innocent's Song
The Flowering of the Thorn
have all been recorded on the album *West Country Christmas* by Johnny Coppin. Red Sky Records.

Keep the Flame
Past Three A Clock
Over the Snows
High in the Heaven
On Christmas Day
Mummers' Jig
Drive the Cold Winter Away
Wassail!
have all been recorded on the album *A Country Christmas* by Johnny Coppin. Red Sky Records.

Christmas Eve has been recorded on the album *English Morning* by Johnny Coppin and is also one of the extra tracks on the CD of *A Country Christmas*.

Winter has been recorded on the album *English Morning* by Johnny Coppin and on the *Gloucestershire Collection (Forest & Vale . . . /English Morning)* CD.

DISCOGRAPHY

Roll on Dreamer 1978. Reissued 1992. Red Sky RSKC 102
No Going Back 1979. Rola R 002
Get Lucky 1982. Starward SWL 2003
Forest and Vale and High Blue Hill 1983. Red Sky RSKC 015 / RSKCD 015/107
  Poems of Gloucestershire with settings of Ivor Gurney, Leonard Clark, Laurie Lee, F.W. Harvey, John Drinkwater, Frank Mansell, Eva Dobell and John Haines.
Line of Blue 1985. Red Sky RSK 106/RSKC 106.

English Morning 1987. Red Sky RSK 107/RSKC 107 / RSKCD 015/107. Songs of Gloucestershire and beyond, with settings of Ivor Gurney, John Masefield, Leonard Clark, W.H. Davies, Frank Mansell, John Drinkwater, Edward Shanks, Eva Dobell, and Edward Berryman.
Edge of Day (with Laurie Lee) 1989. Red Sky RSK 108/RSKC 108/RSKCD 108. A seasonal anthology in words and music – a tribute to the poetry of Laurie Lee.
The Glorious Glosters (with Band of Glos. Regt) 1990. Red Sky RSK 109/RSKC 109. Includes settings of Gurney, Harvey, Clark, and Mansell.
Songs on Lonely Roads – The Story of Ivor Gurney (with David Goodland) 1990. Red Sky RSKC 110. A 90-min musical drama telling the story of one of Britain's finest composers and war poets through his letters and poems.
West Country Christmas 1990. Red Sky RSKC 111/RSKCD 111. Includes settings of Charles Causley, Thomas Hardy, and Leonard Clark.
Force of the River 1993. Red Sky RSKC 112/RSKCD 112 Songs written in the border counties and includes a setting of Margery Lea's 'On a Hill in Shropshire'.
A Country Christmas 1996. Red Sky Records RSKC 114/RSKCD 114. Includes settings of Charles Causley and Eleanor Farjeon, and songs by Jackson Browne, and Robbie Robertson.

All albums on Red Sky Records are available at good record shops (via Topic, CM and ADA Distributors) and by Mail Order direct from Red Sky Records. For a catalogue and price list please write to Red Sky Records, P O Box 27, Stroud, Glos. GL6 0YQ, UK.

If you would like to join the mailing list for news of future concerts, album releases, and books, then please send your name and address to Red Sky Records.

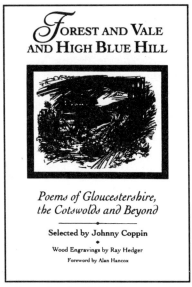

Paperback, £7.99, illustrated

Hardback, £14.99, illustrated

ORDER FORM

Quantity	Title	Price
	P&P	£1.00
	Total	

Please charge £ _____ to my credit card

Cards accepted – Access, Visa, Mastercard, Eurocard. Enter card number below

| | | | | | | | | | | | | | | | | | | | | |

Card Expiry Date _____ Signature _____

Name and Address

_____

_____

_____

Or send cheque payable to The Windrush Press
The Windrush Press Ltd,
Little Window, High Street,
Moreton-in-Marsh,
Gloucestershire, GL56 0LL
Tel: 01608 652012/Fax: 01608 652125